Absolute Press

Fiona Beckett

Beyond Baked Beans

REAL FOOD FOR **STUDENTS**

First published in Great Britain in 2003
by **Absolute Press**
Scarborough House
29 James Street West
Bath BA1 2BT
Phone 44 (0) 1225 316013
Fax 44 (0) 1225 445836
E-mail info@absolutepress.co.uk
Website www.absolutepress.co.uk

Illustrations by Andy Pedler
Photography by Flyn Vibert

A catalogue record of this book is available
from the British Library

ISBN 13: 9781899791835

Printed and bound in Slovenia

For more information visit
www.beyondbakedbeans.com

Beyond Baked Beans

REAL FOOD FOR **STUDENTS**

CONTENTS

INTRO

Why knock baked beans? Let me hasten to say I've nothing against them personally. In many ways they're perfect student food – cheap, tasty, filling and reasonably healthy. but if that's going to be the sum total of your culinary achievement for the next three years you're going to have a pretty boring time.

Being able to cook has many, many advantages; which are – in the order they are most likely to appeal to you:

a) it will make you more popular
b) it will make your money go further
c) it will make living away from the comforts of home more bearable
d) having a varied diet will make you a lot healthier and less likely to pick up every
    bug that's going

Being able to cook well, and by that I mean producing food that looks good as well as tasting good, has the added bonus of being enjoyable and creative – a way to relax.

Of course, I don't think you are going to spend your whole time in the kitchen. Like anyone else there are times when you need to make yourself something to eat in minutes instead of hours, other times when the pressure is to produce a cheap weekday supper and still others when you want to show off a bit. Which is why I've divided the book into three main sections: Fuel, Favourites and Feasts.

What I hope is that there will be something in it for you whatever stage of cooking you're at or get to over the three years you're at university. And that you'll find some recipes in it that will remain firm favourites even after that.

BASICS

This is what you need to get started; the crucial kit, the must-have store cupboard ingredients, smart ways to shop and eat and invaluable advice that will safeguard your equipment, accommodation and friendships.

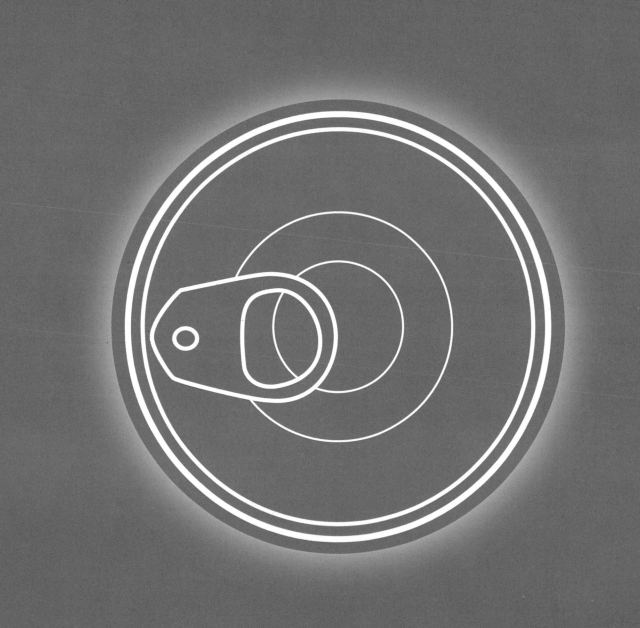

If you've already done some cooking at home the big difference you'll notice about cooking in a student kitchen is the lack of kit. Those endless bowls, pans, knives and labour-saving machines you take for granted are simply not there. At least not unless you bring them with you.

Look on the bright side – if there are fewer things to cook with there are fewer things to wash up. And there's no point in acquiring too much stuff of your own or it'll simply get nicked.

Obviously you can't actually cook properly unless you have the basics and if you're keen you'll want to add to these. That doesn't have to cost a bomb. Chances are your parents want to chuck out some stuff anyway. Or that they'll be so anxious about how you're going to look after yourself when you leave home they'll kit you out. (You can always point out magnanimously that if they give you their old toaster/kettle/mixer they can treat themselves to a new one.)

You can acquire other things – extra knives, forks, spoons, plates and glasses – bit by bit from charity shops or car boot sales. Discount stores like TK Maxx are good sources of inexpensive kitchen equipment such as pans. Or simply wait for the sales.

MUST-HAVES

When I say 'must-have' someone must have it – not necessarily you.

LARGE (PREFERABLY NON-STICK) FRYING PAN

Not just for fry-ups but for quick meat and fish cooking too. It should be deep enough to be able to do a stir-fry, unless you're also going to buy a wok (*see* p12). Incidentally, your frying pan is less likely to stick if you don't use washing-up liquid on it. Just rinse it under the hot tap as soon as you've finished using it and wipe it with kitchen towel.

LARGE LIDDED SAUCEPAN OR STEAMER

The main purpose of which will probably be cooking pasta and making large batches of soup. The advantage of steamers – which are not too expensive these days – is that they have an inbuilt colander which means you can strain the pasta when you've finished cooking it. You can also steam veggies and fish.

SMALL/MEDIUM NON-STICK PAN

For scrambling eggs, heating up soup, making sauces, boiling eggs... (you could actually do with two but one will suffice).

LARGE ROASTING DISH

For that Sunday lunch you're going to make. Or for anything you want to bake in the oven. Like roast potatoes.

MUST-HAVES

MEDIUM-SIZED MICROWAVEABLE DISH
Obviously essential if you have a microwave.
But it should do double duty in a conventional
oven, if you want to make a crumble for example,
or something like a macaroni cheese.

CHOPPING BOARD
Plastic is easier to clean – and cheaper –
so I'd go for that.

SMALL KNIFE FOR PREPARING VEGETABLES,
LARGE KNIFE FOR CUTTING/CARVING MEAT
Both knives should be kept sharp –
a knife sharpener would help but isn't cheap.
An old-fashioned hardware shop or kitchen shop
might sharpen them for you. Or even a friendly
butcher provided you buy from him occasionally.

PAIR OF KITCHEN SCISSORS
For cutting the rind off bacon and opening those
plastic packets you can't open with anything else.

CAN OPENER
Not all cans have ring pulls.

CORKSCREW
Obviously. Get an old-fashioned twist-and-pull
one. Plastic corks will destroy a decent one.

MUST-HAVES

WOODEN SPOON
Preferably two.

FISH SLICE OR SPATULA
For lifting fish, fried eggs or anything else flat
and floppy out of frying pans. Get one with a
long handle if you intend to use it with a wok.

GRATER
For cheese (cheddar on the large holes,
Parmesan on the small ones), carrots, fresh
ginger. The square box-style type is easier to use.

LARGE MIXING BOWL
AND A SMALL MIXING BOWL
A large one will double as a salad bowl;
the small one is ideal for mixing up salad
dressings (unless you have a convenient jam jar),
beating eggs, etc.

MEASURING JUG
Graded with solid measurements as well as
liquid ones.

PEPPER MILL
Freshly ground pepper makes the world of
difference. It doesn't have to be one of those
flashy wooden jobs – a plastic one will do fine.

KITCHEN KIT

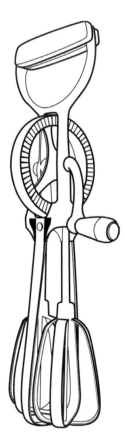

WOULD COME IN USEFUL

Whilst not necessary, these could all further save you time and energy.

ICE-TRAY
Certainly if you're into cocktails. Nice for cold drinks during exam time too.

GARLIC CRUSHER
You can of course chop it by hand but a crusher is quicker and less smelly.

LEMON SQUEEZER
You can stick a fork in the cut side of half a lemon and wiggle it while you squeeze but you'll get more juice out of a squeezer.

WOK
You can cook a surprising number of things in a wok if you haven't got or don't want to switch on an oven. One with a lid is useful (though you can use a sheet of foil). You can buy them cheaply in Chinese supermarkets – though this type may rust if you don't wash and dry them immediately after use.

COLANDER AND/OR A SIEVE
If you don't have a steamer you'll need something to strain your pasta (you can also use it as a steamer if you fit it on top of a saucepan and cover it with a lid). A sieve is useful for rice or for straining sauces that have lumps in them (not that yours will, I'm sure).

WOULD COME IN USEFUL

MEASURING SPOONS
Not vital but they're not expensive and do make following recipes easier.

SCALES
Depends how precisely you like to measure things. A safety net.

TIMER
Unless you're amazingly well organised.

BAKING SHEET
Useful for heating up pizzas and for cooking pies and cookies.

ROLLING PIN
Again, useful if you want to make or roll out pastry. But you can use a (clean) wine bottle at a pinch. Also useful for bashing escalopes.

SERRATED BREAD KNIFE
If you're into unsliced bread. Quite useful for cutting tomatoes too.

WOULD COME IN USEFUL

ROTARY WHISK
If you want to whip cream or egg whites for meringues. For basic whisking (eggs, salad dressings) a fork will do.

A VEGETABLE PEELER
Not essential but it does make the job easier.

A POTATO MASHER
Ditto. Worth getting if you're heavily into mash.

METAL TONGS
Very useful for turning sausages, bits of chicken, etc.

A CHEESE SLICER
Yes you can use a knife but a slicer makes it much easier to cut fine slices for sandwiches and as a topping for toast.

A BISCUIT TIN
To stop your biscuits going soggy.

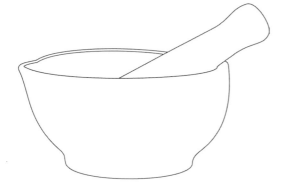

GET SOMEONE TO GIVE YOU

If you're knocking together a uni wish-list, you could do far worse than to include some of these.

KETTLE AND A TOASTER
Though there's always a danger that everyone will bring one. Worth checking first.

HAND-HELD MIXER, BLENDER OR FOOD PROCESSOR
Basically something to blitz soups. Hand-held blenders are the best value and take up least space. Blenders get a smoother result and can be used for smoothies too. A food processor will also make pastry and chop ingredients like vegetables and nuts. Depends how ambitious a cook you are.

A CAST-IRON GRILL PAN
A heavyweight ridged grill pan for quick, low-fat cooking. You get the grill really hot (about 3-4 minutes on the hob) lightly smear or spray your food with oil then quickly sear it either side. Gives a real barbecue flavour – but creates a lot of smoke. (Follow the cleaning tips for 'frying pan', *see* p10.)

GET SOMEONE TO GIVE YOU

A CONTACT GRILL
A bit like a sandwich toaster without the sandwich indents so you can also grill burgers and other flat bits of meat and fish on it.

A PESTLE AND MORTAR
If you want to do some Jamie-style bashing. Useful if you're into Thai, Indian or Moroccan cooking – anything which involves grinding up spices. Fun to use too. You'll find them cheapest in Asian supermarkets.

A COFFEE MAKER
Real coffee is an expensive habit but once you've got the bug nothing else will do. It doesn't need to be electric though – go for a cafetière if you like a lighter style of coffee, an Italian stove-top coffee pot if you want a strong espresso hit.

OTHER KITCHEN BASICS

A round-up of all those other things which should be to hand in any student kitchen.

FOIL, CLING FILM, KITCHEN TOWEL, PLASTIC BAGS (for keeping fresh herbs in), OVEN GLOVES, APRON, PLASTERS (for when you inevitably cut yourself), FIRE BLANKET OR EXTINGUISHER (just in case...), WASHING-UP LIQUID, SCOURERS/WASHING-UP BRUSH, TEA-TOWELS (enough to always have a clean one), SPONGE CLOTHS, KITCHEN CLEANER, BRILLO PADS (for stuck-on gunk, but no good for non-stick pans), BIN BAGS, FRIDGE THERMOMETER (to tell if your fridge is cold enough; obviously, turn it up if it isn't).

AND FOR THE TABLE...

FORKS, KNIVES, SPOONS, TEASPOONS, SERVING SPOONS, LARGE PLATES, SIDE PLATES, MUGS (vast quantities of), EGG CUPS, SOUP/CEREAL BOWLS, AND A COUPLE OF SERVING PLATES/BOWLS.

IN YOUR KITCHEN CUPBOARD

No student these days can afford a well stocked store cupboard but there are ingredients without which you can't cook at all (salt and cooking oil for example) and others you should acquire if you want to eat well (assuming you do or you wouldn't have bought this book). It also makes sense – however tough it may be on the budget – to buy staples like pasta or tinned tuna when they're cheap. More on this in the next section on smart shopping.

The stars of your store cupboard however should be herbs, spices and other flavourings that will transform the other cheap ingredients you have to buy into really tasty food. Which ones you pick depends on your own preferences – whether you're mad about chilli for example or more into Italian – I can only tell you what I wouldn't want to be without. Don't panic by the way if you get to the middle of a recipe and find you haven't got exactly the right ingredient. You can almost always substitute something else. Just pick them up as you can afford them.

SECRET WEAPONS

Six ingredients I'm never without.

FRESH PARSLEY OR CORIANDER
They may seem like an indulgence but fresh herbs make all the difference to the look, taste and texture of your food. Buy them if you can in an Asian, Turkish or Middle-Eastern grocer where you'll find bunches twice the size and half the price of those you get in supermarkets (though you will need to wash them before you use them, *see* p34). Flat-leaf parsley generally has a better flavour than curly parsley, but is often more expensive.

A COUPLE OF FRESH LEMONS AND A LIME
A squeeze of lemon or lime juice lifts almost any dish. Once cut, keep them in the fridge wrapped in cling film. Unwaxed fruit is better, particularly if you want to use the zest. They're juicier too, but they don't keep as long and you can often only buy them in packs of four which is really annoying. To get the maximum juice out of a lemon or lime, warm it by rolling it on a work surface or chopping board under the palm of your hand for a few seconds or microwave it for 20 seconds on a very low setting.

SECRET WEAPONS

GARLIC
Essential for any Mediterranean-inspired recipe, especially tomato-based sauces. You need it for stir-fries and curries too. Remember a clove is one section of a head, not the whole thing (my first major mistake when I started cooking). If you don't like handling garlic you can buy fresh garlic paste but it's pricey. Incidentally garlic should be kept out of the fridge.

FRESHLY GROUND BLACK PEPPER
Light years away from the beige powdery kind. Add during and after cooking.

A CHUNK OF PARMESAN
Or rather Grano Padano which is pretty well the same but comes from outside the officially recognised area so is slightly cheaper. Freshly grated Parmesan just tastes so much better than the stuff you buy in sachets or cartons and although it's pricey a little goes a long way. Buy it from an Italian deli if you can.

EXTRA VIRGIN OLIVE OIL
For salad dressings and drizzling over vegetables or pasta. Again, it's expensive so buy when there's a special offer. Use cheaper sunflower oil for frying.

SECRET WEAPONS

I also wouldn't want to be without...

CUMIN
My favourite spice. It's tangy flavour just conjures up the flavours of Morocco and the middle east. You can buy it ground or as whole seeds (which are fabulous dry-roasted). Like all spices it's much cheaper in Asian shops than in supermarkets. Use it on its own or as the base of a Moroccan Spice Mix (*see* p35).

OREGANO
One of the most versatile of herbs, it won't give your food that horrid dried herb flavour. Invaluable for mediterranean salads and pasta sauces. If you can't find it use a pinch of dried marjoram or thyme.

SMOKED PAPRIKA (PIMENTON)
This Spanish paprika has a fabulous smoky flavour – it comes in two strengths: Dulce (sweet) and Piccante (hot). If you can't find (or afford) it some chopped chorizo (a wonderful spiced Mediterranean sausage) plus a little bit of ordinary paprika will give you a similar flavour. Or use some mild chilli powder.

THAI SWEET CHILLI SAUCE
Much more exciting than ketchup but you can use it the same way. Cheapest from Chinese supermarkets. (*See also* Cucumber and Sweet Chilli Salsa, p64.)

IN YOUR KITCHEN CUPBOARD

SECRET WEAPONS

SOY SAUCE
Useful for stir-fries. I prefer light to dark although Kikkoman is a good brand without additives.

FRESH GINGER
Adds a hot, lemony kick to stir-fries and other Asian dishes. Buy a chunk, keep it wrapped in the fridge then peel and grate it as you need it.

MARIGOLD VEGETABLE BOUILLON POWDER
Much, much better than any stock cube I've tried. Really natural tasting. A 150g tub should last you a good half-term.

MARMITE
Even if you don't like it as a spread buy it as a gravy base or for stock (see p78).

DIJON MUSTARD
Mainly for a classic vinaigrette but you can also whip up classy tasting sauces with it. Get someone to bring you back some from France if you can. It's a fraction of the price it is here.

RUNNY HONEY
Useful as a sweetener or as a sweet-sour glaze.

SECRET WEAPONS

Handy to have to hand...

HALF A DOZEN EGGS
A PACK OF CHEDDAR OR OTHER
  HARD CHEESE
A PACK OF BACON
A COUPLE OF ONIONS
TOMATO PASTE
  (adds richness to tomato sauces; if you don't have any you can always use a little tomato ketchup)
A TIN OF TOMATOES OR A CARTON OF
  PASSATA OR CREAMED TOMATOES
A PACK OF DRIED SPAGHETTI OR OTHER
  PASTA SHAPES (preferably Italian)
A PACK OF BASMATI RICE
  (much more flavour than easy-cook)

A COUPLE OF TINS OF CANNELLINI BEANS
OR CHICKPEAS
A CAN OF TUNA
A GOOD CURRY PASTE AND/OR
CURRY SAUCE (Patak's are the most authentic)
TABASCO OR OTHER HOT CHILLI SAUCE
A JAR OF MAYONNAISE
(for salads and sandwiches)
PLAIN UNSWEETENED YOGHURT
(to accompany fresh fruit or stir into dips,
dressings or curries)
A PACK OF INSTANT MASH
(flakes rather than powder)
A COUPLE OF PACKS OF GOOD
INSTANT NOODLES
A SMALL PACK OF PLAIN FLOUR

AND THE BASICS YOU SHOULDN'T FORGET

AN INEXPENSIVE OIL FOR COOKING
Sunflower or rapeseed for preference.

BUTTER
Even if you don't use it as a spread butter has
a great flavour for cooking. If you can buy it on
promotion use spreadable butter which kills two
birds with one stone.

RED OR WHITE WINE VINEGAR

FINE SEA SALT
Tastes much, much better than table salt.

I'm assuming you've already thought of coffee,
tea, sugar, fresh and long life milk, bread,
breakfast cereal, some kind of butter or low-fat
spread, jam....

Shopping is as much a part of good eating as being able to cook well. But shopping on a budget takes a lot more ingenuity than when you have unlimited funds. If you're well off it's easy – so long as you can recognise good produce. On a food budget of around £25 a week you need sharp eyes and a lot of low cunning.

The standard advice is to go to markets and supermarkets round about closing time when you can pick up a bargain. And that's perfectly true except you know and I know you've got better things to do on a Saturday afternoon. Or most of the time you have anyway.

So how can you survive? Well, this should help.

12 WAYS TO SAVE YOURSELF MONEY

1 STEER CLEAR OF
FASHIONABLE INGREDIENTS...

That means almost anything that's been recently demonstrated by a telly chef – fresh pasta, basil, pesto, pinenuts, mascarpone... (these ingredients are usually Italian by the way). Basically if everybody wants to buy something, supermarkets can get away with charging more for it.

There are often perfectly good substitutes – dried pasta for instance (no self respecting Italian would use anything else unless it was home-made). Frozen spinach instead of those overpriced bags of baby spinach leaves. Caerphilly- about half the price of fashionable Feta cheese. Pearl barley instead of risotto rice.

Watch out too for 'added-value products' such as tinned tomatoes with garlic or herbs which cost almost twice as much as those that don't. And don't taste as good as adding your own seasoning.

2 ...AND FASHIONABLE COUNTRIES

Products from unglamourous countries such as Germany are often cheaper than those from sexy Italy. German salami, frankfurters and Quark (low-fat cheese) for instance are all really good value. Cypriot hummus and olives are the lowest price around.

3 BE FLEXIBLE

Go shopping with an open mind rather than a set idea of what you want to buy. There's bound to be at least one good Buy One Get One Free offer or some fresh produce that's reduced because it's reached its sell-by date. Obviously there's no point in stocking up excessively even if the budget will stretch to it but if it's something which you normally buy like pasta or tuna take advantage. There may also be offers on things you can't normally afford like New Covent Garden soups. This is particularly true at certain times of year – for instance there are always big reductions on smoked salmon in the run up to Christmas, Easter and Valentine's Day, on lemons before pancake day and on soy sauce and stir fried veg before the Chinese new year.

4 BE AWARE OF WHAT THINGS COST

That might sound blindingly obvious but supermarkets rely on the fact that we're not that price-conscious. You can be sure that if they're cutting prices on salmon or steak for instance they're making it up somewhere else – usually on something you buy regularly and unquestioningly such as cucumbers, onions or bananas. Not all special offers are as good as they look. A free cauliflower if you buy a packet of mange-tout is not a bargain if mange-tout is £1.89.

The keenest offers tend to be on the pack sizes people buy most often – it's often cheaper proportionately to buy a 400g tin of tomatoes than a 200g can for example. On the other hand it's cheaper to buy a big pot of yoghurt than individual cartons. Get used to checking the unit price on the shelf stickers under the product which will enable you to compare the price per kilo or 100g. (I know that sounds a bit anorakky and you won't always have time to do it but in time you get to know what things should cost).

5 IT ALSO HELPS TO BUY INGREDIENTS THAT ARE IN SEASON

Again that might sound obvious but it can sometimes be hard to tell when you can buy strawberries in December and leeks in July. And when some foods like tomatoes, cucumber, broccoli and peppers are available all year round. But if you're buying in a market you'll really notice the difference.

Cheaper in winter
   root veg (carrots, swedes, parsnips), cabbage and greens, leeks, citrus fruit (oranges, grapefruit and lemons), apples

Cheaper in summer
   lettuces, cucumbers, tomatoes, peppers, new potatoes, courgettes, asparagus, strawberries, raspberries, cherries, peaches, grapes

6 AVOID CONVENIENCE FOODS

If someone else does the work for you, whether it's washing a lettuce, dicing your meat, grating your cheese or making your pasta sauce or gravy, you pay. A lot. Sometimes that may be worthwhile – it would cost you far more to chop up the ingredients for a stir-fry for instance than to buy a bag of ready prepared veg, especially for one. And bagged salads can be a boon. But on the whole if you're prepared to use a knife, a grater or simply wash a few leaves, you're going to save yourself a lot of money. That also goes for buying fresh produce. You'll pay quite a bit less for things like apples or onions if you buy them loose than if someone has pre-packed them for you.

7 TRY OWN BRANDS

You may be addicted to Kellogg's or Bird's Eye but at least give the supermarket own-brand version a go. You may not always be convinced. Personally, I'm less keen on supermarket own-brand pasta which seems to end up soft and gluey when it's cooked and always buy Italian brands (despite what I've said about Italian food, dried pasta is not overpriced). But I can happily put up with own-brand yoghurt.

8 USE LOCAL SHOPS WHEN YOU CAN

Fresh herbs and spices for example are much cheaper from an Asian, Turkish or Cypriot grocer than a supermarket. Afro-Caribbean grocers are a good source of cheap veg. Buy ingredients for oriental dishes like soy or chilli sauce from a Chinese supermarket. Parmesan and Mozzarella will be cheaper from a specialist Italian deli. If you pass a local butcher, fishmonger or baker on the way home, use them.

9 PLAN

That may sound as if it contradicts 'be flexible' but it's a question of making the best use of what you've got. Half a dozen eggs for instance can make you three meals (scrambled egg, spaghetti carbonara and a big egg and cress roll); a tin of tuna can make a salad and a pasta sauce if you have the strength of will not to pick at it and store it in the fridge. It's always worth cooking extra potatoes, pasta and rice to provide the basis for a quick meal (hash, pasta salad, egg-fried rice...).

10 SHARE

Admittedly it's more practical in a house than in hall but pooling your resources makes it a lot easier to budget. Easier said than done I know as not everyone is into cooking and some people won't pull their weight. But at least get them to chip in if you cook for them.

11 MAKE YOUR OWN SANDWICHES

Or salad, or whatever it is you like for lunch. Ok it doesn't look as cool but it'll probably save you a fiver a week at least.

12 BUY YOUR TAKEAWAYS FROM THE SUPERMARKET

Supermarket pizzas are a fraction of the price of most delivery services and now that many supermarkets are open 24 hours you can get them at any time. OK you've got to heat them up but that shouldn't be too big a deal. Their curries are often better quality too.

BARGAIN BUYS

MEAT

It's better to buy cheap cuts from well treated (at least free range) animals than prime cuts from intensively reared ones. (Chicken drumsticks are a classic example. Burgers another. Buy the best you can afford). Apart from mince, stewing cuts like shin (leg) of beef are good value, cheaper than ready prepared casserole steak. Pork is inexpensive, especially chops (people don't like bones these days, but maybe you don't either). Same applies to offal such as liver and kidneys (though I do urge you to try the liver recipe on p68). Frozen meat can be fine, especially New Zealand lamb (shoulder is good for roasting). Tinned corned beef and ham are great value. So are frankfurters.

Look out for offers on mince, chicken drumsticks and thighs, sausages, ham, and streaky and middle bacon (middle is a combination of back and streaky – both are better value than back). Any bacon is cheaper if you're prepared to cut off the rind yourself – look out for packs of bacon 'bits' or offcuts.

FISH

Fresh fish can be quite pricey – unless you have a friendly fishmonger. Exceptions are mackerel, herrings, sardines and trout but then there's the bone issue.

Best value is canned fish – especially tuna, mackerel and sardines – and frozen which is often fresher than fish that's been hanging around on a counter (it's still not cheap but it's more likely to be on special offer). Frozen kippers are a snip.

Look out for offers on salmon (and occasionally smoked salmon), frozen prawns and tinned tuna.

FRUIT AND VEG

The hardest things to shop for because prices fluctuate so wildly. Some frozen veg (peas and spinach for instance) are better value than fresh. Certainly cans can be (see below). Lettuces are much better value than salad in bags so long as you're prepared to wash them. And cress is a steal. On the fruit front, kiwi fruit always seem to be cheap.

Look out for offers on tomatoes, broccoli, peppers, avocados and most fresh fruit.

BREAD

There will always be a cut-price sliced loaf. It will always taste of cotton wool. Don't go there. Buy a large loaf and cut it yourself. French sticks are cheaper than sexier Italian breads like ciabatta and flat breads.

Look out for offers on pitta bread, ciabattas and wraps.

CHEESE

Despite the fact that Cheddar dominates the cheese counter it can be cheaper to buy regional British cheeses like Caerphilly, Double Gloucester, Red Leicester and Wensleydale. If you like blue, Danish Blue is cheap – use sparingly because of its strong flavour. In fact strong cheeses are always better value because you don't need to use so much. Herb and garlic-flavoured soft cheese is inexpensive too if you buy own label. So is Quark, a light German soft cheese.

Look out for offers on Cheddar, Brie and Camembert.

YOGHURT, CREAM AND BUTTER

Maybe it's because so many people are slimming, but cream is amazingly inexpensive – particularly single cream. Fromage frais is cheaper (and lower in calories) than sexier crème fraîche. Butter is often cheaper than spreads these days and easy to spread thinly if you keep it at room temperature. Buy plain yoghurt in big pots.

Look out for offers on butter and cream.

HERBS

Go for the biggest bunches you can find. Most herbs are not worth buying in pots, thyme and rosemary excepted.

READY MEALS

There are times we all resort to ready meals. If you're cooking for one it can actually be cheaper than buying your ingredients from scratch. On the other hand you don't get a lot for 99p and many meals cost a lot more than that. However, you can often bulk them out with extra meat or veg to make them feed two or three. Very few cook-in-sauces are worth the money though. And most taste unpleasantly synthetic.

Look out for offers on fish and chicken fillets in breadcrumbs, chicken kiev, fishcakes, fish pie (hard work to make yourself), lasagne (ditto, though almost never as good as home-made), stuffed pastas like ravioli, good quality Italian pasta sauces (such as Sacla), good curry sauces (such as Patak's) and Swedish meatballs.

CANS

Though some admittedly are foul, cans are hugely underrated as a source of good cheap food. Without baked and other kinds of beans, chickpeas, tomatoes and tuna you will not survive. Canned fruit is worth buying too, especially pears and grapefruit.

Look out for offers on tinned tomatoes, tuna, and olives in tins rather than jars.

SMART EATING

If you're on a tight budget it's not easy to eat healthily I admit. But then it's not that easy on an unlimited budget either. Basically it needs a conscious effort on your part, an effort that may seem just too tedious to make.

The reason you should is not simply to do with your long term health – it's hard to focus on the possibility that you may suffer from osteoporosis when you're 70 – but about your health right now. If you don't eat a well balanced diet you stand a much greater chance of getting ill. Not seriously ill but subject to the kind of succession of colds and other bugs that can make you feel tired, listless and depressed.

It can also of course make you less attractive. Overweight. Spotty. Greasy-haired.

Convinced? Here's how to do it.

THE 4 CRUCIAL FOOD GROUPS

The key to healthy eating is to incorporate something from within each of these groups every day. Yes, even fat has a part to play.

1 FRUIT AND VEG

5 portions a day is the amount the health tsars recommend but I reckon 4 is a more realistic target. If you always have some fruit juice or a piece of fruit for breakfast, a portion of veg or salad for lunch and supper and a piece of fruit some time during the day you'll achieve it but for most of us it takes a conscious effort.

The key is to think about it every time you prepare food. If you make a fry-up, add a tomato. If you make a sandwich cram in some cucumber or lettuce. If you heat up a lasagne or other ready meal make sure you have a salad too (although the tinned tomato in lasagne counts, certainly in a home-made version). If you have a nibble of cheese, accompany it with an apple, pear or a stick of celery. Use fresh herbs wherever possible in your cooking.

If the cost daunts you remember frozen and canned fruit and veg count too. The ones in fruit or natural juice are obviously healthier than the ones in syrup or with added sugar.

2 BREAD, POTATOES, PASTA AND RICE

A crucial source of energy that you may be tempted to skip if you're trying to lose weight. (But don't – just go easy on the butter or rich sauces you put with them). Obviously wholemeal products are better (higher in fibre and B vitamins – the ones that stop you feeling stressed) but if you don't enjoy the taste don't torture yourself. Even bog standard white bread is fortified with calcium. About 50% of your diet (5-6 helpings a day) should be made up of carbohydrate but that doesn't mean you have to live off sandwiches and pasta. Grains like couscous, bulgur wheat and polenta count too. As do breakfast cereals (which are also fortified with B vitamins and iron).

3 RED MEAT, CHICKEN, FISH, EGGS AND VEGGIE ALTERNATIVES

Protein provides iron and zinc which are vital for cell health and renewal. The easiest way to absorb it is by eating meat but vegetarians can get it from beans and lentils, nuts, seeds, soy products, egg yolks, fortified breakfast cereals and dark green veg like spinach and cabbage. Even meat-eaters should vary their sources of protein and not just rely on bacon sarnies to do the job. Remember the amount of actual meat in many processed foods and ready meals can be quite low. Aim for 2-3 small servings a day• – and a couple of portions of oily fish like mackeral or tuna a week (good for your heart).

If you are vegetarian drinking a vitamin C-rich drink like orange or cranberry juice with a meal or following it with fruit, like oranges, strawberries or kiwi fruit will help you absorb iron more effectively.

• You don't need as much as you might think. A skinless chicken breast will actually provide almost all your daily protein requirements. A small 50g chunk of cheese would provide about a third of it.

4 MILK, CHEESE AND YOGHURT

Important for the calcium they contain which keeps your teeth and bones healthy. You should aim for 2-3 servings, some of which will obviously be accounted for by the milk you have in tea and coffee. The downside is that full-fat or sugary versions can also pile on the pounds so stick to semi-skimmed milk, low-fat cheeses such as Quark and fromage frais and plain unsweetened yoghurt if you're trying to keep your weight down but don't skip them altogether. (Plain yoghurt is more flexible than flavoured yoghurt anyway as you can also use it in savoury dishes.) Vegans should make sure they have enough non-dairy sources such as calcium-enriched soya milk and tofu, green leafy vegetables, brazil nuts and dried apricots.

LEARN TO LOVE...

LENTILS Rich in B-vitamins, iron and fibre
LIVER Rich in iron
SARDINES, MACKERAL (AT LEAST
  TRY IT SMOKED) AND OTHER OILY FISH
  Rich in omega 3 fatty acids which offer
  protection against heart disease
SPINACH, WATERCRESS AND OTHER DARK
LEAFY VEG Rich in iron, beta carotene, vitamin C
CARROTS Rich in beta-carotene and vitamin A
KIWI FRUIT More vitamin C than oranges
MANGOES Rich in fibre and vitamin C and E
TOFU High in protein, helps lower cholesterol
WHOLEMEAL BREAD Rich in iron, selenium
  and other minerals

SHOULD I TAKE VITAMIN SUPPLEMENTS?
If you know your diet is deficient in crucial vitamins
such as C and B (which can easily happen if
you're a smoker) I think you should – especially
if you're going down with a cold. Sure, it's much
better to eat the right foods but if you haven't
been eating that well supplement your diet till
you're back on track. If you do feel seriously
run down you should of course consult a doctor.

LIQUID REFRESHMENT

I'm not going to get preachy about how much
you should drink other than to remind you that
the recommended daily maximum is 3 units for
women and 4 for men. And that's really, really
easy to exceed. A small (125ml) glass of 13.5%
Chardonnay is about 1.8 units alone and most
glasses you pour will be a lot bigger than that.
One cocktail or a double vodka and you're almost
at the limit. Alcohol is also fattening – anything from
about 90 calories to 120 calories a glass so don't
be surprised if a lot of partying piles on the pounds....

What you *should* be drinking is water. Lots of it –
about 2 litres or 8 large glasses – a day. Coffee and
tea don't count (they contain caffeine which increases
the heart rate and can make you feel jittery) but fruit
squashes and herbal and fruit 'teas' are OK.

SNACKING ISN'T BAD...

Or it needn't be provided it doesn't consist solely
of fatty or sugary foods. Supplies of nuts, raisins
and other dried fruits like apricots provide iron and
other essential vitamins and minerals, a low-fat
yoghurt will boost your calcium intake, a banana
will give you energy. Keep a supply of sliced
peppers, celery and carrots in the fridge for
when hunger strikes or dunk in hummus for
a more substantial snack.

If you are going to attempt to eat healthily you need to know how to cook and prepare a few different veg, so you don't bore yourself witless eating peas and carrots all the time.

ASPARAGUS

Cheap in season April-May. Cut off the woody end of the stem about a third of the way up. Place in a microwaveable dish with a little water and a damp piece of kitchen towel (run a sheet under the tap and shake off the water), or use cling film. Microwave on high for 3-4 minutes. Rest for a minute. (Or place in a saucepan with some boiling water half way up the stems, cover with a sheet of foil and steam for 3-4 minutes.) Serve hot with melted butter or allow to cool and use in a salad. **NB** Asparagus makes your pee smell weird. Don't worry – you haven't got a deadly disease. **1 bunch will serve 2 as a main dish.**

BEANS (GREEN)

Cut off the stalk and the wiggly bit at the end. Leave small (dwarf or Kenya) beans whole otherwise cut into thick slices. Place in a saucepan and cover with boiling water. Add salt, bring back to the boil. Cook for about 7-10 minutes until you can easily stick a knife through them. Drain in a colander or sieve and run cold water over them to keep them green. Return to the pan with a little butter or olive oil and crushed garlic and heat through gently for 3-4 minutes. **A 250g pack will serve 3-4.**

BROCCOLI

Cut each head of broccoli into small florets. Rinse. Either microwave (see asparagus method, opposite) or steam (see 'Steaming', opposite page) for 4-5 minutes. Or stir-fry adding a little water and garlic and soy sauce to taste. **1 head will serve 2-3 as a vegetable.**

CABBAGE AND GREENS

Remove the outer leaves then cut into quarters, removing the tough white stalk in the centre. Shred the rest of the leaves finely and rinse. Cook in a little boiling salted water for about 2-3 minutes, stirring occasionally. Drain and serve with plenty of butter and black pepper. Or stir-fry (see broccoli, above) – a better method for oriental greens like pak choi. **Half a cabbage will serve 3-4.**

CARROTS

Scrub clean and peel if necessary (supermarket carrots are usually washed). Cut off any leaves or stalks. Slice into rounds or diagonal slices (you may need to halve or quarter them if they're particularly large). Heat a little butter or oil in a large saucepan and add a pinch of ground coriander or cumin and a pinch of sugar. Stir the carrots around in the melted butter then pour over half a glass of water, cover with a lid or foil and cook for about 10-12 minutes. New carrots (which tend to be sold with their leaves still on) will take a little less. You can also steam them. **Allow 1 medium sized carrot per person.**

CAULIFLOWER

Cut the white, creamy florets off the stalk, cut into even-sized pieces and either steam or cook in boiling water (about 8 minutes either way). Serve with Classic Cheese Sauce (*see* p106) or double the sauce used for the Gooey Cheese Fondue Potatoes (*see* p71).
A medium cauli' serves 3-4.

CORN ON THE COB

Cut off the stalk and tear off the outer husk. Plunge each cob into a large saucepan of boiling water (don't salt it – it makes them tough) and cook for about 7-8 minutes. Drain and smother with soft butter. **Allow 1 cob per person.**

COURGETTES

Easily go soft or soggy so best briefly fried or steamed (*see* below). Trim each courgette at the ends and slice. Grate the courgettes coarsely and throw them into a frying pan in which you've heated a tablespoon of oil and a good chunk of butter. Stir-fry for 1 minute then season with salt and pepper. Add some chopped fresh parsley if you like. **Allow 1 medium courgette per person.**

Steaming

- My favourite way of cooking veg with a short cooking time, like asparagus, broccoli, cauliflower, courgettes and mange-tout. If you don't have a steamer, put them in a metal colander over a pan of boiling water covered with a lid or a piece of foil.

CUCUMBER

Whether or not you peel cucumber is a matter of taste. Ditto whether you eat the seeds though they do make a dish more soggy. But the technique that makes them taste best is to salt them.

An Incredibly Slimming Cucumber Salad

$1/3$ of a cucumber
$1/2$ tsp salt
1 tbsp seasoned rice vinegar
A little salt and pepper to season

Peel the cucumber, slice thinly and place on a plate. Sprinkle with the salt, put another plate on top and weight it down with a tin. Leave it for half an hour. Put the cucumber in a sieve and rinse with cold water. Pat dry with kitchen towel. Pour over the seasoned rice vinegar and season with a little salt and pepper. Excellent with cottage cheese, tinned tuna or salmon. Serves 1.

LEEKS

Trim off any roots and the coarse green leaves off the top of the leek (about a quarter of the way down). Slice thickly in rounds then wash thoroughly under running water. (If you buy them from a market stall they're likely to have quite a bit of earth still on them.) Stir-fry in a little oil and butter for 5-6 minutes until soft, then season. You can use leeks in the place of onions.
Allow 1 medium-sized leek per person.

LETTUCE

(*See* Un-Bagged Salad, p57.) Add a salad dressing just before serving (*see* p56). Store any leftover leaves in a plastic bag in the fridge – they should keep for up to two days if your lettuce was fresh in the first place. **One small round lettuce will serve 2-3, a larger cos or iceberg lettuce about 4-6.**

MANGE-TOUT/SUGARSNAP PEAS

Easy. Rinse and microwave or steam for 2 minutes. (Sugarsnap peas will take 3 minutes.) **A small pack will serve 2-3.**

MUSHROOMS

Small white button mushrooms are best eaten raw in a salad or as part of a stir-fry. Just wipe clean and slice. Bigger, fatter portabella mushrooms are better baked or grilled with garlic butter (*see* p159). **A small pack of mushrooms will serve 2. With big mushrooms you need 1-2 a head.**

PARSNIPS

Trim each parsnip at the top and bottom and peel. If they're large cut into quarters then cut out the woody core. Best as part of a dish of roast vegetables (see below) or as a mash – cook in boiling, salted water until soft (about 15 minutes), drain thoroughly then whizz in a food processor with butter and a little cream. Season with black pepper and a little grated nutmeg if you have some. You can also boil them for just 5 minutes then drain and grill them, trickling over a little runny honey. **Allow 1 medium-sized parsnip each.**

Roast Winter Vegetables

• For four people cut up two medium to large potatoes, carrots, onions and parsnips into even-sized chunks. Lay in a roasting tin and pour over a good glug of olive oil and mix well so the veg are thoroughly coated. Tuck 4-5 smashed garlic cloves in between and a few sprigs of rosemary if you have some. Roast at 200°C/400°F/Gas 6 for about 45 minutes to an hour, turning them half the way through.

PEAS

Check the instructions on the packet. No point in shelling peas unless you're a masochist. **You need about 50g of peas per person.**

POTATOES

The simplest way of cooking potatoes is to boil them. You can peel them or not as you prefer (generally I would with older potatoes and not with new potatoes), if they're old cut them into even-sized pieces – halved or quartered depending on size – cover them with cold water and bring to the boil then cook for about 20 minutes until you can stick a knife into them without any resistance. Drain and add a knob of butter and some chopped parsley and/or chives if you have some. New potatoes are better cooked in boiling water, and only take about 10 minutes. (*See* also **MASH**, p110; baked potatoes, p70; and roast potatoes, p129-31.) **You need about 3-4 small, 2 medium or 1 large potato per person.**

SPINACH

Spinach comes in microwaveable bags these days but it's pricey. If you buy it loose, tip the leaves into a sinkful of cold water and wash thoroughly. Pull off the stalks and central rib of any particularly large leaves. Drain off the water and press the spinach down into a large lidded saucepan. Place over a low heat and cook until the leaves start to collapse. Turn over and cook for a couple of minutes, then drain thoroughly in a colander or sieve. Return to the pan with a good chunk of butter, reheat and season with pepper. **500g of spinach will serve 2-3 people.**

SPROUTS

Cut across the base and remove the outer leaves. If the sprouts are very big cut a cross in the base to help them cook more quickly. Cover with boiling water, add salt and bring to the boil. Cook for about 8-10 minutes until you can stick a sharp knife through them. Drain, return to the pan and add a knob of butter. (See also Hot Buttered Sprouts with Almonds, p133.) **500g sprouts will serve 4-5 people.**

TOMATOES

Two issues: Are they ripe? (Don't bother if they're not.) And do you mind the skin? If you do, simply make a small cut near the stem end, put them in a bowl and pour over boiling water. Leave them for a minute then drain and rinse them in cold water. The skin should come away easily.

Magic Tomato Salad

The magic consists of the fact that this salad dresses itself if made with sufficiently ripe tomatoes.

2-3 really ripe tomatoes (i.e. soft without being squishy)
2 tbsp olive oil
Salt and pepper
2 tsp vinegar
1 tbsp fresh parsley (optional)

Pull the stalks off the tomatoes and slice finely. Place in a bowl, season with salt and pepper and pour over the olive oil. Give the bowl a good shake and leave it for 10-15 minutes which should draw out the juice from the tomatoes. Sprinkle over the vinegar, add the parsley and mix together. If you like, you could also add some finely chopped onion. Serves 1.

HERB AND SPICE LOW-DOWN

There are tricks to using herbs and spices effectively, the main thing to remember being not to overdo it. You don't necessarily get more flavour by adding more ingredients, you just get a muddled one.

CHOPPING FRESH HERBS

Most herbs need to be chopped before you add them (except basil, which is better torn by hand, and chives and dill which are easier to snip with scissors). You need to pull the leaves off the stalks (especially plants with woody stalks like rosemary, mint and thyme). Even if they're from the supermarket it's a good idea to give the sprigs a good rinse or wash in cold water first and shake them dry.

Lay the leaves in a pile on a chopping board. Take a large sharp knife and cut them roughly. Then, holding the tip of the knife on the board with your left thumb and forefinger (or right one if you're left-handed) and the knife handle in your right hand, move the blade up and down and backwards and forwards across the herbs until they are finely chopped.

STORING

Herbs generally keep best in a plastic bag in the salad drawer. The exception is coriander, which is better stored in a tall glass (a beer glass is ideal) or a jam jar full of water (particularly if you buy it loose from an ethnic grocer). Pull a plastic bag over the top and secure it round the outside of the glass with a rubber band. Keep it in the fridge and take it out and wash it as you need it, changing the water at least every other day That way a big bunch should last you a week. Basil is the exception: it won't last more than a couple of days even if kept in the fridge.

DRIED HERBS

Dried herbs have a very concentrated flavour so use them sparingly – about $1/3$ to $1/2$ the amount of fresh herbs you would use (see recipes). You can get more flavour out of them by rubbing them betweeen your thumb and fingers as you add them. They need replacing every six months or they begin to taste stale. Refill boxes and packets (especially own-brand ones) are significantly cheaper than branded jars.

DRIED SPICES

You can either buy spices whole or ready-ground. Ground spices are obviously more convenient but the advantage of whole ones is that they keep better and you get a more intense flavour when you crush them. The easiest way to do this is to pound them, Jamie-style, with a pestle and mortar or in a bowl with the end of a rolling pin. If you have neither, lay them out on a crumpled piece of foil and run a can backwards and forwards over them until they break up. Spices I grind regularly include black peppercorns, cumin and coriander seeds, and cardamom, a fragrant Indian spice that tastes heavenly in milk puddings (see Cardamom Rice Pudding with Shaved Mango, p154).

ROASTING SPICES

This is another way of bringing out the flavour of spices, especially cumin seeds. You don't have to do it in the oven – simply put the spices in a dry frying pan over a low heat and warm through, shaking the pan occasionally till they begin to change colour and give off a spicy aroma.

SPICE BLENDS

You can also buy ready-blended spice or 'masala' mixes (such as the East End Balti masala mix I use for the Vegetarian Samosa Pie – see p156). They tend to be subtler and more fragrant than basic curry powder but sometimes less effective than using spices individually. The one I use most often is a Moroccan-style blend of spices I make up myself which you'll find in several recipes including Moroccan Spiced Fish with Coriander and Couscous (see p120).

Moroccan Spice Mix

2 heaped tsp ground cumin (about 5g)
2 level tsp ground coriander
1/2 level tsp turmeric
1/2 level tsp hot pimenton (see p7) or paprika

Mix the spices together and store in a sealed jar. Seal the open packets of ground spices with a paper clip or roll over the top of the packet and fasten it with a rubber band so they keep in good condition for the next batch. Makes enough for 2-3 recipes.

HERB AND SPICE PASTES

Now widely available and a good way of buying hard-to-find ingredients like lemongrass or ones that you don't much enjoy preparing like garlic, chillies or ginger. The well-known brands can be expensive but you can find cheaper examples in Asian shops. Basil is quite effective as a paste (better than dried) but coriander less so (use fresh instead). You can also buy curry pastes and substitute them for masala mixes. The Thai green curry and red curry pastes are also good, especially if bought from a Thai or Chinese supermarket. Once opened, store any pastes in the fridge. Check the label to see how long they will keep.

FRESH CHILLIES

Generally it's best to remove the seeds, which are what makes chillies so hot. Cut them in half lengthways then scrape out the seeds and white pith with the tip of a teaspoon. Chop the chillies finely.

Chilli alert!

If you rub your eyes – or any other sensitive bodily part – after preparing fresh chillies it will hurt like hell. Always wash your hands immediately after handling them. If you should eat a chilli that's too hot, milk or rice will douse the fire better than water.

HOW NOT TO POISON YOUR FRIENDS

There are an awesome number of cases of food poisoning every year, most of them perpetrated by dodgy restaurants and fast food traders.
If you don't want to add to those statistics you need to be at least vaguely aware of what constitutes food hygiene.

 Always wash your hands thoroughly before starting to prepare food. With soap. And dry them with a hand towel or kitchen towel rather than your tea-towel.

 Keep your working surfaces clean.
Or use a clean chopping board if they're not. Give them a good blitz every couple of days with an anti-bacterial cleaner.

Keep the sink clean and free from teabags, potato peelings, leftover pasta and other grot.

Wash your tea-towels regularly and replace the washing up brush and/or scourers before they get too squalid.

Keep the food you store in the fridge wrapped or covered – partly to avoid cross contamination, partly to stop them drying out.

☠ Don't store fresh and cooked meat side by side or put fresh meat or fish where it can drip onto cooked food (no wonder so many people are vegetarian). Wash any utensils or chopping board you have used for preparing raw meat before using them for anything else.

☠ Don't refreeze frozen food that has thawed, especially ice cream.

☠ If you're using frozen chicken or other joints defrost them completely before cooking them.

☠ If you cook something to eat later or have perishable food left over cool it then refrigerate it (NEVER put warm food in the fridge). If you're going to eat it hot always reheat it thoroughly – that means simmer it for at least 5 minutes.

☠ Make sure your fridge is set at a cold enough setting for the amount of food it has in it. (Afraid there's no other way to check than buying a fridge thermometer). Defrost and clean it thoroughly at least once a term.

☠ Refrigerate perishable food as soon as you can after buying it. Don't lug it round warm lecture rooms and coffee bars.

☠ Store the contents of half-finished tins like canned tomatoes or fruit in china, glass or plastic containers. Tins that are left open to the air can corrode.

☠ Get rid of anything that smells rank or shows obvious signs of decay – spots of mould, furry growths or generally unappealing squishy bits. Also potatoes that have sprouted or developed green patches. And anything that has passed its eat-by date. If in doubt, chuck it out.

HOW NOT TO POISON YOUR FRIENDS

HOW LONG THINGS KEEP IN THE FRIDGE

Obviously it depends when and where you bought them and how quickly you put them away. Produce bought loose, especially from small shops will generally need to be eaten sooner than pre-packed produce which has been chilled, though it also depends on the sell-by date. If you buy things cheap because they've reached or are nearing the end of their shelf life you should generally eat them the same day.

Eat within 24 hours
High-risk foods such as shellfish and other fresh fish, mince, offal, pre-prepared salads, stir-fries and beansprouts.

Eat within 1-3 days
Chicken and other meat, sausages (if wrapped), mushrooms, soft fruit such as strawberries, leftovers.

Eat within 4-6 days
Soft cheese, yoghurt, milk, tomatoes and other fresh veg.

Eat within a week to 10 days
Bacon and ham (though consume within a couple of days once you open the pack) hard cheese, eggs.

Store for up to a month or more
Butter and spreads (check the use-by date). Frozen foods (but ice cream should never be refrozen once thawed).

And remember...
Always read the instructions on jars once you've opened them. Many products such as mayonnaise and cook-in sauces need to be kept in the fridge.

KEEP OUT OF THE FRIDGE

Garlic, onions and melons (will taint the other food you've got stored there, especially butter). Bananas and avocados go black and soggy. Potatoes are best stored in a paper bag. If you buy them in a plastic bag, tear it open so the air can get to them.

FOOD ALLERGIES

Quite a few people are allergic or intolerant to ingredients these days, most commonly wheat and dairy products made from cow's milk. But it's nuts and shellfish (even if fresh) that can make them seriously ill. Most of them will be aware of the risk but never include either ingredient in a dish without telling your friends you've done so. Especially peanuts which can be fatal.

...NOR SCALD, ELECTROCUTE, AND SET FIRE TO THEM

More fires start in the kitchen than any other room in the house – usually when someone just wanders off and forgets that they've left something on the hob. Apart from that...

 DON'T buy dodgy second-hand appliances with frayed cords.

 DON'T leave kitchen towel, tea-towels or oven gloves near the hob where they can catch fire.

 DON'T cook with floppy sleeves.

 DON'T cook when you're legless.

DON'T leave pan handles sticking out from the stove.

 DON'T leave the hob, oven or appliances like sandwich toasters on when you've finished cooking.

 DON'T use a metal or foil container in a microwave.

DON'T let electrical leads sit or dangle near water.

 DON'T leave your toaster full of crumbs and your grill pan clogged with fat. It's asking for a flare-up.

AND WHAT TO DO IF THE OIL IN A PAN CATCHES FIRE

Throw a damp towel over it to exclude the air (wring it out under the tap). Never throw water on a fire. If it's out of control get everyone out of the kitchen, shut the door and call 999.

IT'S BLINDINGLY OBVIOUS BUT...

 Read any new recipe through in full before you start cooking. Laying out and preparing the ingredients you need also helps.

 If you're buying pre-packed foods make sure you read the instructions.

 Most recipes in this book can be halved or doubled but spices and seasonings don't usually need to be changed that much. Use a little bit less or a little bit more, tasting as you go.

 Vegetables take different time to cook. Account for this when you're timing a meal.

 Ovens – particularly student ovens – are temperamental and can be slightly hotter or cooler than the norm'. (In a gas oven the top of the oven is always hotter than the bottom.) If you find your food is generally overcooked use a setting lower than I recommend. If it's undercooked turn it up a setting. Don't keep opening the oven door while food is cooking.

 Always preheat the oven before you put the food in.

 Remember what time you put the food on to cook (a timer helps).

 Don't use the same cooking fat continuously – it will taste rank. And don't pour fat down the sink – it'll block it. Cool it then pour it into a disposable container like a yoghurt pot and put it in the bin.

Plates and pans are easier to wash when you've finished using them rather than three days later. If you have got to that stage soak them first.

It's much easier (and more hygienic) to wash up in hot water than lukewarm or cold.

 If you use a metal spoon, scourer or brillo pad on a non-stick pan you'll ruin it.

DO MEASUREMENTS MATTER?

Some of the best cooks cook without measuring anything so why bother with measurements? Because while chefs are used to measuring things by eye, feel and taste, if you haven't cooked much before you're more likely to succeed if you know roughly how much of what to put in. That said you don't have to take what I say as gospel. If I recommend using 400g of onions and you only have 350g that's not going to make a big difference. But doubling the quantity of a strong flavoured spice like chilli powder is.

Some measurements are approximate, leaving it up to you how much to add – one *or* two cloves of garlic for instance. Others take account of the fact that you may not have a set of measuring spoons, a measuring jug or scales. When I say teaspoon an ordinary teaspoon will do but keep it level (i.e. the ingredients should be level with the rim of the spoon). A rounded teaspoon would be slightly more than that. There are 3 teaspoons in a tablespoon. If you haven't got a tablespoon use a large serving spoon. This is quite a useful way to measure out butter, particularly soft butter. The amount you would cut off with a tablespoon is about 15g.

Sometimes with herbs or greens like spinach I'll recommend a handful. Which is exactly that – the amount you can pick up and hold in your hand (without trying overhard to cram it in). An ordinary mug is a reasonably good measure for liquid. If you fill it up to the level you'd normally fill it for a coffee, it'll hold about 225-250ml.

Recipes that are suitable for vegetarians are marked with a 🍁 symbol. Recipes that are suitable for vegans are marked with a 🍁🍁 symbol.

So far as cooking terms are concerned I've tried to keep it simple but if a phrase has slipped in you don't understand or if something goes horribly wrong you can e-mail me at **info@beyondbakedbeans.com**.

FUEL

There are times when you need to eat quickly.
On your own or maybe just making enough for you
and a flatmate. It's certainly not worth putting on the
oven so these are mainly things you can make in a
saucepan or a wok. Some of them are more complicated
than others, but you can do them all in under 30 minutes.
And they'll taste a lot better than pot noodles. Promise.

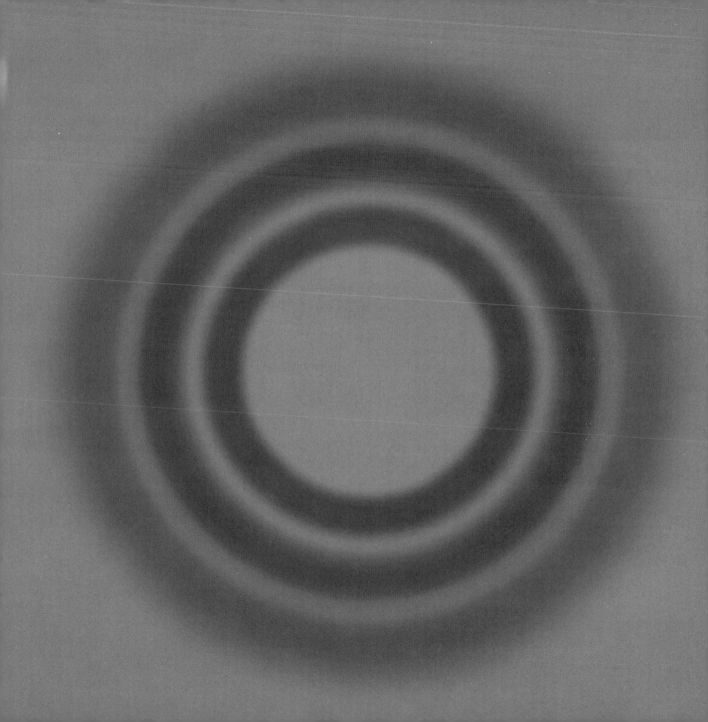

Pasta has to be the starting point of any student cookbook. The easiest, cheapest quickest meal there is.

Given that there are dozens of different ready-made pasta sauces you might wonder why bother to make your own. Simple: they're cheaper and they taste better. Fresh herbs are always nicer than the dried ones they use in jars.

You may well know how to cook pasta already but if not here's how, followed by two easy tomato sauces, and tomato and pasta go together like... well, tomatoes and pasta.

PASTA FOR ONE

*The quantity of pasta depends on how hungry you are.
The Italian brands are best; don't bother with fresh.*

100g-125g of dried pasta

Boil a full kettle and tip the water into a large pan. Bring back to the boil, add the pasta and about 1/2 tsp salt, stir then cook for the time recommended on the pack. To check if the pasta is done hook a strand or piece out of the pan and bite into it. It should be neither hard nor soft and soggy. Drain it in a colander or sieve, saving a little of the cooking water to add to your sauce. Return the pasta to the pan then toss with enough sauce just to coat it lightly. Don't drown it.

! The most common mistake people make is not using enough water. You need a litre for every 100g of pasta you cook.

THE EASIEST EVER PASTA SAUCE ✪
Serves 1 (plus 1)

This makes enough sauce for two meals – a plate of pasta plus enough left over to make huevos rancheros (see p53) or anything else for which you need a bit of tomato sauce.

2 tbsp olive oil
1 clove of garlic, peeled and crushed
1 400g tin of tomatoes in their own juice
salt, pepper and sugar to taste
2 tbsp chopped fresh parsley
Parmesan or Grana Padano, freshly grated

Heat the oil in a large frying pan. Add the garlic. Tip in the tin of tomatoes and crush with a fork or a wooden spoon. Season with salt, pepper and a pinch of sugar and simmer for about 10 minutes till thick and jammy. Stir in the parsley and cook for a minute. Spoon half the sauce over a plate of freshly cooked pasta and grate over some Parmesan.

You can also add

- Half a can of tuna and either a few black olives or 1 tbsp of capers rinsed and roughly chopped (this tastes better without cheese).
- A chopped red pepper fried in a little olive oil and a little chilli sauce.
- A small aubergine, cubed and shallow-fried.

TAGLIATELLE WITH SWEET TOMATO AND FRESH BASIL SAUCE V Ve Serves 2-3

Delicious but only worth making in season (i.e. summer) when tomatoes are ripe and cheap. The sauce also tastes very good with gnocchi or rice.

2 tbsp olive oil
250g cherry tomatoes
1 small clove of garlic, peeled and crushed (optional)
250g pack of tagliatelle
Sea salt, sugar and freshly ground black pepper
6-8 basil leaves, torn into 2-3 pieces

Heat the oil for a couple of minutes in a large frying pan. Add the tomatoes and fry for about 2-3 minutes until the skins start to split. Cover the pan with a lid or with foil and cook for about 4-5 minutes until they're quite soft. Crush them thoroughly with a fork or wooden spoon so the juices run out, turn the heat down, add the crushed garlic.

Stir well and cook for about 8-10 minutes until the sauce has begun to thicken. (If you want you can sieve the sauce at this point to get rid of the tomato skins.) Meanwhile cook the tagliatelle for the time recommended on the pack. Drain well and return to the pan. Season the sauce with a little salt and sugar if needed and plenty of freshly ground black pepper, add the basil then pour it over the pasta and mix well.

You can also add

- A small cup (about 100g) of frozen peas.
- 125g fresh or frozen prawns.
- A spoonful of double cream or crème fraîche.

Cream and butter have been virtually outlawed by the health police but they're a lot better for you – and cheaper – than most ready-made sauces. If you're completely skint you can always serve pasta with a little butter and grated cheese like the Italians do (though admittedly they probably don't use bog-standard Cheddar).

PENNE WITH COURGETTES AND LEMON 🍁 Serves 1

A light, fresh pasta sauce – really good for summer.

100g dried penne, fusilli or other short pasta shapes
2 medium courgettes (about 200-250g)
A good slice of butter (about 25g)
1 small clove of garlic, peeled and crushed
3 tbsp double cream
1-1½ tbsp lemon juice
2 tbsp chopped fresh parsley
Salt and freshly ground black pepper
Freshly grated Parmesan or Grana Padano

Bring a pan of water to the boil, add ½ tsp salt then cook the pasta for the amount of time recommended on the packet. Meanwhile cut the top and bottom off the courgettes and grate them coarsely. Heat a large frying pan or wok, add the butter, then stir-fry the courgette and garlic for 2 minutes until just cooked through. Drain the pasta, saving a little of the cooking water and return to the pan. Pour over the cream and lemon juice, tip in the courgettes and chopped parsley and fork through the pasta. Add a spoonful or two of the cooking water to lighten up the sauce. Check the seasoning adding salt, pepper and extra lemon juice to taste then serve sprinkled with grated Parmesan.

- Instead of courgettes you could use lightly cooked asparagus or broccoli.
- Or make a luxury version with leftover smoked salmon or smoked salmon trimmings (see p168).

What to do with leftover pasta
- If you're cooking pasta shapes it's worth making extra for a pasta salad. Simply rinse the leftover pasta in cold water as soon as you've drained it, then mix with a little finely chopped onion, cucumber, red pepper, a dollop of mayo and ½ a tin of tuna.

RICOTTA AND SPINACH TORTELLINI WITH LEMON BUTTER SAUCE 🌿 Serves 1-2

When pricey stuffed pastas like tortellini or ravioli are on special offer take advantage to make this ultra-quick and easy sauce.

250g pack Ricotta and Spinach Tortellini
A good slice of butter (about 25g)
Juice of 1 lemon (2-3 tbsp)
2 heaped tbsp finely chopped parsley or – better still – parsley and chives
Salt and freshly ground black pepper

Follow the pack instructions for boiling the pasta (about 1-2 minutes from the time the water comes back to the boil). Drain in a colander or large sieve. Melt the butter in the same pan and add the lemon juice. Return the pasta to the pan and heat through for a couple of minutes. Add the fresh herbs, toss the pasta and serve on warmed plates or in bowls.

SPAGHETTI CARBONARA WITH PEAS Serves 1-2

Home-made is always better than a shop-bought carbonara sauce and dead easy.
You can even leave out the peas – and the onion – and it'll still taste good.

1 tbsp cooking oil
6 streaky bacon rashers, rinded and chopped or 125g bacon bits
1 small or $1/2$ a medium onion, peeled and finely chopped
75g frozen peas, soaked for 2 minutes in boiling water or microwaved
2 large eggs or 3 medium eggs
2 tbsp freshly grated Parmesan or Grana Padano plus extra for serving
A handful (about 125g) dried spaghetti
Salt and freshly ground black pepper

Heat the oil in a frying pan over a medium heat and fry the bacon until the fat begins to run. Add the onion, turn the heat down low and fry for another 5 minutes or until soft. Stir in the peas and leave the pan over a very low heat. Beat the eggs with 2 tablespoons of the Parmesan and season with freshly ground black pepper and a little salt. Cook the spaghetti in plenty of boiling water – following the instructions on the pack. Once it's cooked, drain it thoroughly, saving a bit of the cooking water and return it to the pan, off the heat. Quickly tip in the bacon, onion, peas and beaten eggs and mix thoroughly so the egg 'cooks' in the hot pasta. Add a spoonful or two of the cooking water, season again with black pepper then serve immediately with extra Parmesan.

Noodles should really be as popular as pasta. They're just as cheap, quicker to cook and can be combined with a stir-fry just as easily as pasta with a sauce (which is why I've coupled them together). They're also extremely versatile – you can serve them dry like pasta or wet like soup. Maybe that's the problem. There are just too many recipes from too many cooking traditions (Chinese, Japanese and Thai, to name just three) involving too many different types of noodles to be able to get to grips with them easily. (Oh yes, and they're slithery too.) Add to that the fact that most of the ready-made sauces for noodles are dire and it's not surprising they have a bad name.

Persevere though; if you've travelled in Thailand or even visited noodle restaurants here like Wagamama or Busaba Eathai you'll know just how good – and sustaining – they can be. So, to start, a quick guide to the most common types of noodles:

Pot noodles
Unless already addicted, avoid at all costs. Not the best way to feed yourself for the next 3 years.

Instant noodles
Flavoured ones are not a great deal better than pot noodles with the exception of authentic Japanese brands (see recipe below). Unflavoured ones (such as Blue Dragon Express) are quite useful though they don't have as good a texture as egg noodles.

Egg noodles
These look and taste very similar to pasta. Best for stir-fries.

Soba noodles
Made partly from buckwheat, these are the most tasty noodles – similar to wholewheat pasta. Good for Japanese-style soups and salads.

Rice noodles
The kind to use in Pad Thai and other Thai stir-fries and soups. Useful if you're wheat-intolerant.

! Remember, noodles tend to stick together much more than pasta. You'll need to keep separating them with a fork whilst they're cooking.

THREE-MINUTE NOODLES 🍁 Serves 1

Proof that even instant noodles can be made to taste good... so long as they're Japanese.

1 packet instant Japanese soba noodles with sauce

Add any or all of the following
- A little freshly grated ginger and/or garlic or half a teaspoon of ginger and/or garlic paste
- A good squeeze of lemon or lime
- Some chopped fresh coriander leaves
- Some sweet chilli sauce

Make up the noodles according to the instructions on the packet. Once hot, stir in as many of the other ingredients as you fancy. Eureka!

SPICY, SOUPY CHICKEN NOODLES
Serves 1-2

Now there are so many hot chicken counters in supermarkets it's easy to pick up a couple of drumsticks really cheaply. If not, buy some cold flavoured roast chicken.

2 hot and spicy, Chinese or barbecued chicken drumsticks or a chicken thigh
4 spring onions or 1 small onion, peeled and finely sliced
1 head of pak choi (bok choy) or ½ head of spring greens or ½ small green cabbage or ½ pack of chopped greens
75g soba noodles
2 tbsp oil
1-2 cloves of garlic, peeled and finely sliced
A pinch of five spice (optional but good)
250 ml chicken or vegetable stock made with ½ stock cube or 1 tsp Marigold vegetable bouillon powder
1½ tbsp soy sauce
Hot pepper sauce to serve

Cut the chicken meat off the drumsticks. Cut the root off the spring onions and cut away half the green top. Slice thinly in diagonal slices. Wash the pak choi or cabbage leaves, removing any tough stalks and slice thickly. Cook noodles in boiling water following instructions on pack (break them up with a fork to stop them sticking together). Drain and rinse with cold water. Heat a wok over a moderate heat, add the oil and fry the sliced onions, garlic and five spice, if using, for a couple of minutes. (If you use an ordinary onion fry it first then add the garlic.) Add the chicken, cook for a minute then add the greens and stir-fry for 2-3 minutes until they begin to wilt. Add 3-4 tbsp of the stock and the soy sauce and fry for another couple of minutes until the greens are cooked. Add the noodles to the wok together with the rest of the stock and heat through for about two more minutes. Serve in bowls with hot pepper sauce to taste.

♥For a veggie dish replace the chicken with 125g of sliced mushrooms.

! With stir-fry dishes it really helps to get the ingredients ready before you start.

SWEET CHILLI NOODLES WITH PRAWNS Serves 1-2

Although this Thai style noodle dish appears expensive because of the sweet chilli sauce and fish sauce, if you're into Thai food you'll get plenty of use for them.

100g egg noodles or a pack of instant noodles
2 tbsp cooking oil
4 spring onions, trimmed and thinly sliced (see previous recipe) or 1 small onion, peeled and thinly sliced
1-2 cloves of garlic, peeled and finely sliced
A small chunk of fresh ginger, peeled and coarsely grated or 1/2 tsp of ginger paste (optional)
1/2 a small pack of mange-tout sliced into 3 or about 75g frozen peas
100g frozen prawns
1 1/2 tbsp fish sauce
1 1/2 tbsp fresh lime or lemon juice
1 1/2 tbsp sweet chilli sauce
About 2 tbsp fresh coriander, roughly chopped (optional)

Cook the noodles in boiling water following the instructions on the pack. Drain and rinse with cold water. Heat a wok or large frying pan and pour in the oil. Add the spring onions, garlic and ginger if using, fry for a minute then add the mange-tout, fry another 2 or 3 minutes, then the prawns. Stir-fry until the prawns and mange-tout are cooked then add the fish sauce, lime or lemon juice and the sweet chilli sauce. Add the drained noodles to the pan with a couple of tablespoons of water and heat through. Add the fresh coriander and serve.

• You could substitute 125g broccoli florets (divided up small) for the mange-tout.

♥For a veggie version use 125g mushrooms instead of prawns. Replace the fish sauce, lime juice and chilli sauce with 1 1/2 tbsp soy sauce.

EXTREMELY EASY STIR-FRY Serves 2

With so many pre-prepared stir-fries there's absolutely no point in slicing up vegetables yourself. It isn't any cheaper (than the basic mixes anyway) and it's a lot more hassle. The only downside is that you have to eat them within 24 hours which requires a degree of forward planning that doesn't fit easily into the student lifestyle. By the way, don't feel you have to buy a ready-made sauce to go with it – soy sauce will do fine.

2 tbsp oil
300g bag of stir-fry vegetables
1 cooked chicken breast, skin removed and cut into thin strips (optional)
2 tbsp light soy sauce

Heat a wok or large frying pan until it begins to smoke. Pour in the oil and immediately tip in the vegetables and the chicken. Cook for a couple of minutes, stirring them so they don't burn.

Add about half a small glass (50ml) of water and cook until evaporated. Add the soy sauce and cook for a few seconds more. Taste, adding more soy if you think it needs it. Serve up.

• You could substitute 75g of cashew nuts for the chicken.

Stir-fried veg

• Stir-frying is a great way of preparing quick-cooking veg like cabbage, mushrooms and mange-tout without losing valuable nutrients in the cooking water. You can even cook harder vegetables such as carrots and courgettes in a wok if you grate them first (see p30).

Eggs, let's face it, are a lifeline. They never take more than 10 minutes to cook and for under a pound you can make yourself at least three meals. Strangely, given they're so simple to cook, there's a surprising difference of opinion on how best to do it. Here's what I do anyway.

Boiled eggs

Start with the eggs at room temperature (if you prick the base with a pin it will lessen the risk of them cracking). Bring a small pan of water to the boil. Place each egg in a spoon and lower it carefully into the water. Boil for 3½-4 minutes (medium eggs) and 4-4½ minutes (large eggs) for a yolk runny enough to dunk toast in. (A timer helps.) For hard-boiled eggs continue to boil for 10 minutes in total. Remove the eggs and transfer them to a pan or bowl of cold water. To peel them, crack them gently against a hard surface and peel off the shell under running water.

Fried eggs

Heat a frying pan for a couple of minutes until moderately hot then add 3 tbsp (clean!) cooking oil. Crack the egg(s) on the side of the pan (or on the edge of a cup if you feel a bit nervous about it) and break the egg(s) into the pan. Cook for a couple of minutes then add a small lump of butter to the pan, tilt it, holding the handle and spoon the hot butter and oil over the eggs so the yolks cook thoroughly and the whites puff up. (*See also* the Ultimate Fry-Up, p166.)

Poached eggs

Don't bother unless you have a poacher. They're tricky. (If you have a poacher, simply boil water in the pan, swirl a small lump of butter round each of the cups then slip in the eggs (having cracked them first in a cup). Put the lid on the poacher and cook for about 4-4½ minutes (till the whites are set.)

Scrambled eggs (see p54)

! Use eggs that are as fresh as possible, preferably free-range.

HUEVOS RANCHEROS ('RANCH-STYLE' EGGS)

V Serves 1

This hearty Mexican breakfast dish is one of the best ways of serving fried eggs (think ketchup-plus). The tortillas might sound like an extravagance but they make the dish and you can use the remainder in other ways (see below).

3 tbsp sunflower or olive oil
1 small onion, peeled and
   roughly chopped
1-2 mild green chillies and/or
   1/4 tsp chilli powder or
   cayenne pepper
1 clove of garlic, peeled and
   roughly chopped
1/2 a 400g tin of chopped
   tomatoes or – only if they're
   really ripe – 3 fresh tomatoes
 Salt, for seasoning
1 tbsp chopped coriander
   or parsley (optional)
2 corn tortillas (optional)
2 large free range eggs

Heat a pan over a moderate heat, pour in 2 tablespoons of oil then add the chopped onion, chillies, garlic and tomatoes. Stir well and cook for about 5 minutes until most of the tomato juice has evaporated and the sauce is becoming jammy. Season with salt then stir in the fresh coriander or parsley if using. Tip into a bowl. Rinse the pan clean under the tap, wipe dry then swirl round the remaining oil and wipe off the excess with kitchen towel. Take one of the tortillas and press down in the pan for 30 seconds to warm it through then flip it over and cook the other side. Repeat with the second tortilla. Lay them on a large plate. Fry the eggs as described opposite and place over the tortillas. Spoon the hot salsa on top.

- Instead of making a sauce from scratch you can use the Easiest Ever Pasta Sauce (see p44) and add the onion and chilli.
- You can use the remaining tortillas as a base for other sandwich and toast toppings (see pp72-74), with Chilli Con Carne (see p94) or with chicken, bacon or avocado salads (see p58).

EGYPTIAN-STYLE EGGS WITH CHICKPEAS **V**

Serves 1

This dish is traditionally made with ful medames – *a deliciously spicy brown bean sludge that is regarded as Egypt's national dish but I like it with chickpeas.*

1/2 a 400g can of chickpeas
Salt and freshly ground black
   pepper
1/4 tsp ground cumin
3-4 tbsp extra virgin olive oil
Some chopped parsley or fresh
   coriander (optional)
2 fresh eggs

Rinse the chickpeas in a sieve under the cold tap and put in a bowl. Season with salt, pepper and cumin and pour over 2-3 tablespoons of olive oil. Mash the chickpeas with a fork until they have a rough consistency. Check the seasoning then stir in the parsley or coriander if using. Serve with fried eggs (see opposite).

- Add a little chopped onion or small clove of garlic if you want to make it even punchier.

You can make scrambled eggs two ways – very slowly which will result in them being rich and creamy or much faster which will end up tasting more like an omelette. There's a place for both techniques.

SLOW, BUTTERED SCRAMBLED EGGS WITH HAM Serves 1

2 large fresh eggs
1 tbsp milk
Salt and pepper
1 tbsp soft butter (about 15g)
1 slice of ham, cut into strips

Break the eggs in a bowl and beat with a fork. Add the milk and season with a little salt and pepper. Place a small, preferably non-stick pan on a gas or electric ring set on a very low setting. Add the butter and let it melt then tip in the eggs. Stir them continuously till the mixture starts to solidify (anything from 3-5 minutes) then keep stirring till you have a rich creamy golden mass. Just before they're ready stir in the ham. Serve on hot buttered toast.

• Instead of ham you could add mushrooms. Fry them in the pan first then set them aside while you make the scrambled egg.

STIRRED EGGS WITH CHILLI AND CORIANDER 🌱 Serves 2

This Asian-style egg dish (discovered in Australia) is more a stir-fry than a scramble. It's specially good with naan bread but if you can't find it on special offer just have it with toast.

3 spring onions
1 mild fresh red or green chilli (not the blisteringly hot bird's eye type)
1 tbsp sunflower or olive oil
5 large fresh eggs, preferably free-range
Salt
2 tbsp roughly chopped coriander leaves
1 large or 2 mini garlic and coriander naans (optional)

Trim the roots and half the green tops of the onions, discard, then chop finely. Halve the chilli, scrape out the seeds and chop finely. Heat a pan (preferably non-stick), over a moderate heat add the oil and and cook the spring onions and chilli until soft (about 3-4 minutes).

Beat the eggs and season with salt. Turn up the heat slightly and pour in the eggs. Push them around the pan with a wooden spoon till they begin to solidify then about a minute before they're cooked chuck in the coriander. Warm the naan under a grill or pop in a toaster (halve if necessary to fit). Spoon the eggs onto warm plates and serve with the naan.

POTATO, BACON AND ONION FRITTATA

Serves 2-3
(or 1, plus frequent fridge raids)

Frittatas are a cross between a quiche and an omelette – packed with filling but served flat rather than folded. They are a great way of using up leftovers and can also be eaten cold themselves with salad or as a sandwich filling.

3 tbsp olive or sunflower oil
1 small pack of bacon bits or 6 rashers of streaky bacon or 3-4 rashers of back bacon, rind removed and roughly chopped
2 medium raw or cooked potatoes, peeled and cut into small chunks
1 medium onion peeled and roughly chopped
6 eggs
2 tbsp chopped parsley (optional)
salt and pepper

Heat 2 tablespoons of oil in a frying pan and fry the bacon pieces for a few minutes until beginning to brown. Scoop them out onto a plate without discarding the oil. Add the potatoes and cook over a medium heat for about 5-6 minutes, turning them from time to time until they start to brown. Add the onion and cook for another 5-6 minutes stirring occasionally until both the potatoes and onions are thoroughly cooked. Return the bacon to the pan. Crack the eggs into a bowl, beat lightly with a fork, add the parsley if using and season with salt and pepper. Pour evenly over the vegetables. With a fork lift up the edges of the frittata as it cooks to allow the liquid egg to run over the base of the pan. Leave it to cook for another 4-5 minutes while you turn on the grill, then put the pan briefly under the grill (not too close) to brown the top of the frittata. (If you don't have a grill cover the top of the pan with a lid or with foil so the egg on the top cooks through.) Slide the frittata onto a plate and cut into quarters.

Alternative fillings

- Chorizo, potato and onion: replace the bacon with the same amount of chopped chorizo.
- Green pepper, potato, onion and garlic: add a chopped green pepper and a crushed clove of garlic at the same time as the onion.
- Leek, pea and Parmesan: chop and cook 2 medium-sized leeks in butter (*see* p31), add 100g thawed frozen peas and stir 2 tbsp freshly grated Parmesan into the egg mixture.

It's easy to get in a rut with salads, chopping up whatever you have in the fridge (usually cucumber and tomato) and chucking in a spoonful of sweetcorn but if you think of them more as a meal than the receptacle for your leftovers you'll enjoy them a lot more. It's also worth getting into the habit of having a salad with your main meal as an easy way to up your veg intake. Bagged salads make that easy, though they are admittedly more expensive. Making a dressing from scratch is a good start. Cheap bottled dressings are just as nasty as cheap cook-in sauces. Try to use a decent oil, preferably olive oil. Vegetable and corn oil won't do anything for your salads.

ITALIAN-STYLE OIL, LEMON AND PARSLEY DRESSING Serves 1-2

1 dessertspoon fresh lemon juice
3 dessertspoons olive oil
$1/2$ clove of garlic, crushed (optional)
A little sugar, salt and freshly ground black pepper
1 tbsp finely chopped parsley

Shake the ingredients together in a jam jar or whisk in a bowl with a fork. Suits lettuce, mixed leaf and rocket salads, tomato salads and chickpea salads.

! To whisk with a fork, tilt the bowl towards you and make a quick circular movement with the fork, flicking from the wrist.

FRENCH-STYLE MUSTARD DRESSING (THE CLASSIC 'VINAIGRETTE') Serves 1

$1/2$ tsp Dijon mustard
A little salt and freshly ground black pepper
1 dessertspoon wine vinegar
4 dessertspoons olive oil

Prepare as with Italian-Style. Suits lettuce and dark leaves like watercress and spinach, bean salads and potato salads.

ASIAN-STYLE LOW-FAT DRESSING Serves 1

Rice vinegar is not as acidic as wine vinegar so you don't need so much oil. If you can find organic sunflower oil at a reasonable price, snap it up – it has a much nicer, nuttier taste.

1 tbsp sunflower oil
1 tbsp seasoned rice vinegar
1 tsp soy

Shake or whisk together with a fork. Serve with a crunchy salad or with cold noodles.

UN-BAGGED GREEN SALAD

Although bagged salads are unbelievably convenient they're also about 3 times as expensive than a basic round lettuce (or a cos or iceberg lettuce in season).

1 round lettuce

Remove any damaged and dirty outer leaves, pull off the other leaves and wash them in a large bowl or sink full of cold water. Shake the leaves thoroughly, lay them on a (clean, obviously) tea-towel. Twist the ends of the towel so the leaves don't fall out, and shake them dry. Or pat the leaves dry with kitchen towel. Just before you want to eat the salad pour either the Italian or French dressing (opposite) in a bowl, add the leaves then turn the leaves over in the dressing so that each leaf is lightly coated.

- Store any leftover leaves in a plastic bag in the fridge – they should keep for up to 2 days if your lettuce was fresh in the first place.

! Always toss a dressing at the last minute otherwise your salad will go soggy.

MOROCCAN SPICED CARROT SALAD

Serves 2

Carrots make a great winter salad when other salad veg are expensive.

2 medium carrots, washed and peeled
Juice of half an orange
1 dessertspoon sunflower or olive oil
1/4 tsp Moroccan Spice Mix (*see* p35) or cumin or curry powder
Pinch of sugar
Salt and pepper
1 tbsp chopped fresh coriander or parsley leaves (optional)

Cut the tops and tips off the carrots and grate them coarsely. Mix with the orange juice and spices and season with sugar, salt and pepper. Drizzle with oil and sprinkle with coriander or parsley, if using.

- A good meal for two with a can of chickpeas, drained, rinsed and dressed with the Italian-Style Oil, Lemon and Parsley Dressing (opposite).
- Another way to make this more substantial is to add a chopped stick of celery and some toasted cashew nuts (tossed in a frying pan over a low heat till they start to brown).

AVOCADO SALADS

Avocados have the image of a luxury food but in fact they're quite cheap, particularly if you buy a bag of them. And because they're so rich they're really filling. The only thing you need to be careful about is making sure they're ripe, otherwise they're hard and flavourless.

! To tell if an avocado is ripe press it gently round the narrow end. It should 'give' very slightly.

! The easiest way to halve an avocado is to run a knife round it lengthways, then hold one half in each hand and twist them apart. Scoop out the stone with the end of a knife or spoon, then peel and cut into chunks.

! Don't prepare it ahead: avocados brown as soon as they're exposed to the air.

MOZZARELLA, AVOCADO AND TOMATO SALAD 🍁
Serves 2

For obvious reasons this popular Italian salad is called insalata tricolore – *3 colour salad. Use real Italian Mozzarella – generally cheaper in Italian delis – rather than the Danish stuff which comes in rubbery blocks.*

1 ball of Italian Mozzarella (about 125g)
A small pack of cherry tomatoes (about 250g)
2 medium sized ripe avocados
2 x the Italian-Style dressing (see p56), minus the garlic

Tear the Mozzarella into small chunks, halve or quarter the tomatoes and peel the avocados and cut into large chunks. Mix together lightly in a bowl with the dressing

Try replacing the Mozzarella with...

- 6 streaky bacon rashers fried until crisp and broken into 3. In fact if you're feeling broke leave out the avocado too and add iceberg lettuce. A BLT salad in other words. (Use the French mustard dressing instead of the Italian one.)
- 1 cooked chicken breast, cut into chunks.
- 100g of leftover smoked salmon (*see* p168) sliced into strips.

GREEKISH SALAD

Serves 1

'-ish' because I suggest you use Caerphilly or Wensleydale rather than twice-the-price Feta. 'British Salad' wouldn't sound as sexy!

A good chunk (75-100g) crumbly white cheese such as Caerphilly or Wensleydale
1/4 of a cucumber
5-6 cherry tomatoes
2-3 slices of raw, peeled onion
5-6 black olives (optional)
1/2 tsp dried oregano (optional)
2 tbsp Italian-Style Oil, Lemon and Parsley Dressing (see p56) plus extra salt and lemon to taste

Cut the cheese and cucumber into small chunks. Halve or quarter the cherry tomatoes depending how big they are and roughly chop the onion. Mix together all the ingredients in a bowl with the dressing. Taste and add extra salt or lemon juice if you think it needs it (the original would be quite salty because of the Feta but it's up to you). Good served with (or even stuffed into) warm pitta bread.

CHEESE, CELERY AND APPLE SALAD WITH YOGHURT AND HONEY DRESSING

Serves 1-2

A nice, fresh, healthy-tasting salad to make you feel smug and virtuous.

1 little gem lettuce or half a pack of Iceberg lettuce salad
A good chunk (100-125g) Emmental or Jarlsberg cheese
2-3 sticks of celery, washed and trimmed
1 medium-sized crisp apple (e.g. Braeburn)

For the dressing
1/2 tsp Dijon mustard
1/2 tsp clear honey
1 tsp wine vinegar
1 tbsp sunflower oil or light olive oil
1 1/2 tbsp very low-fat natural yoghurt
Salt and freshly ground black pepper

Trim the base off the lettuce, break off the leaves, rinse under the cold tap and pat dry. Measure the mustard, honey and vinegar into a bowl and whisk together with a fork. Add the oil and yoghurt, whisk again and season to taste with salt and pepper. Remove any rind from the cheese and cut into small chunks. Trim the fleshy white base off the celery and slice thinly. Quarter, core and chop the apple and add to the dressing with the cheese and celery. Spoon over the lettuce.

• You could add some strips of ham if you wanted to make this more substantial.

Even people who don't eat fish make an exception for tuna but I think the tinned version is much nicer (and healthier) cold than hot. And if you're watching your weight buy it in brine rather than oil.

- You can add leftover tuna to tomato sauce or mix with a little chopped onion and celery and a dollop of mayo to fill a roll or sandwich.

EASY ITALIAN TUNA AND BEAN SALAD

Serves 1

The easiest salad in the book – the classic tonno e fagioli.

$1/2$ large tin of tuna (it's invariably better value to buy a large can of tuna than a small one; they're always on special offer)
$1/2$ a small/medium onion, finely sliced
$1/2$ a 400g tin of cannellini beans
2 tbsp Italian-Style Oil, Lemon and Parsley Dressing (*see* p56)

Drain and flake the tuna. Drain and rinse the beans. Mix the two together with the onion and the dressing.

- If you don't like raw onion subsitute 2 sticks of celery, finely chopped.

EASY FRENCH TUNA AND BEAN SALAD

Serves 1

What to do with the other half of your tin... the classic salade nicoise.

$1/2$ a large tin of tuna
A small can of green beans
5-6 cherry tomatoes
5-6 black olives (optional)
2-3 chopped anchovies (optional)
2 tbsp French Mustard Dressing (*see* p56)

Drain and flake the tuna. Drain the beans, rinse under the cold tap and pat dry with kitchen paper. Halve the tomatoes. Mix them all in a bowl with the olives and anchovies if using. Pour over the French dressing and toss together.

- Good with warm new potatoes.
- Obviously you could substitute fresh or frozen beans for the tinned ones – about 75-100g. Once cooked, refresh them under cold water and pat dry.

THAI-STYLE MACKERAL SALAD Serves 1-2

For some reason tinned mackeral isn't regarded as nearly as highly as tuna but it makes a great low-fat salad.

125g can mackeral in brine
Juice of $1/2$ a lime
1 tbsp seasoned rice vinegar
$1/4$ of a cucumber, peeled, deseeded and diced
$1/2$ a red pepper or 5-6 cherry tomatoes deseeded and diced
1 small chilli, deseeded and finely chopped, or a few drops of hot chilli sauce
2 tbsp chopped fresh coriander leaves

Drain the mackeral and break the fillets up into rough chunks. Whisk together the lime juice and rice vinegar. Check for seasoning, adding more vinegar or lime juice if you think it needs it. Mix the mackeral, cucumber, red pepper and chilli together. Pour over the dressing and scatter with fresh coriander.

SMOKED MACKEREL, CUCUMBER AND SOBA NOODLE SALAD Serves 2

Smoked mackerel lends itself really well to this Japanese-style salad.

100g soba noodles or wholewheat spaghetti
1 smoked mackerel fillet
4 spring onions
$1/4$ of a cucumber, peeled, deseeded and diced
2 tbsp Asian-Style Low-Fat Dressing (*see* p56) plus extra rice vinegar to taste
Salt and pepper (unless you use a peppered mackerel fillet)

Cook the soba noodles (*see* p48) or spaghetti, drain and rinse with cold water (break the spaghetti in half before you cook it). With a knife and fork ease the mackerel off the skin and break into rough chunks. Trim the roots and half the green tops off the spring onions, discard, cut the onions into four lengthways, then chop into short lengths. Tip the noodles into a bowl, pour over the dressing and mix well. Add the cucumber, spring onions and smoked mackeral and mix together again. Add a little extra rice vinegar to taste and season with salt and pepper.

• If you have any sesame oil around add a few drops of that too.

If you're watching your weight fish is your friend. Especially if it's steamed or microwaved. If you think that sounds boring, think again. These vibrant Asian flavours are really satisfying and make you feel you've had something much more substantial.

CHINESE STEAMED SALMON WITH GINGER, GARLIC AND SOY

Serves 1

This might sound complicated but once you've mastered the technique – season fish, steam over boiling water – it's a doddle.

1 tbsp light soy sauce
1 small clove of garlic, peeled and crushed
A small chunk of ginger, peeled and finely grated or $1/2$ tsp ginger paste
1 thinnish, boneless salmon fillet, about 125-150g (a tail-end piece is ideal)
2-3 spring onions
A small head of pak choi or 4-5 green cabbage leaves

Mix the soy sauce with 1 tablespoon of water (2 tablespoons if using a dark soy sauce) and add the garlic and ginger. Put the salmon in a shallow bowl and pour over the sauce. Trim the spring onions, cutting off the root and half the green leaves at the top.

Cut each onion lengthways into four. Wash the pak choi or cabbage leaves and use enough to line the perforated tier of a metal or bamboo steamer. Sprinkle over half the spring onions, place the salmon fillets on top then top with the remaining onion. Pour over the soy sauce from the bowl then top with the remaining pak choi leaves. Bring the water in the base of the steamer to the boil, place the steamer tier on top, cover with a lid and cook the fish for about 5-6 minutes until you can easily break off a piece with a fork. Serve with extra soy sauce to taste.

- If you haven't got a steamer use a colander set over a medium-to-large saucepan.
- You can also microwave this dish which will take about 3-4 minutes depending on the thickness of the fish and how powerful your microwave is. Leave the salmon to rest for a couple of minutes before serving.

THAI STEAMED PLAICE WITH COURGETTES

Serves 1

A spin on the previous recipe for Thai food addicts. The list of ingredients may look daunting but if you're into Thai cooking you'll find plenty of use for them (see also p80, p90 and p150).

1 skinless, boneless plaice fillet
1 tbsp fish sauce
A small chunk (about 2cm square) of fresh ginger peeled and coarsely grated
or 1/2 tsp ginger paste
2 stalks of lemongrass
A couple of sprigs of fresh coriander
1 medium to large courgette
3 fresh lime leaves, roughly torn (or dried lime leaves, soaked for 5 minutes in warm water)

Place the fish in a shallow dish. Mix the fish sauce with 1 tablespoon of water, add the grated ginger or ginger paste and pour over the fish. Leave for 10 minutes (or longer if you've time). Peel the outer husk off the lemongrass stalks, chop off the top and bottom and slice the stalk lengthways into four. Remove the leaves from the coriander stalks and roughly chop the leaves. Wipe and thinly slice the courgette and lay half the slices in the perforated tier of a steamer. Sprinkle over a few coriander stalks, strips of lemon grass and pieces of lime leaf, lay the fish over the top then sprinkle with the remaining lemon grass, coriander stalks and lime leaves. Pour over the fish sauce and cover with the remaining courgette slices. Steam for about 4-5 minutes until it flakes easily when you insert a knife. Serve with the fresh coriander sprinkled on top.

- Again, this can be microwaved. Allow about 3 minutes, plus 1 minute standing time.

FISH FINGERS THREE WAYS

The automatic accompaniment for fish fingers – or any other breadcrumbed fish or chicken – doesn't have to be chips. Partner them instead with a healthy salsa, salad or some veg.

WITH CUCUMBER AND SWEET CHILLI SALSA
Serves 2

$1/3$ of a cucumber
1-2 spring onions, trimmed and finely sliced
Juice of $1/2$ a lemon (about $1 1/2$ tbsp)
2 tbsp sweet chilli sauce
a dash of nam pla (fish sauce) or a little salt
1 tbsp roughly chopped coriander leaves

Cut the cucumber in four, lengthways, remove the seeds and cut into small dice. Mix with the onion. Mix the lemon juice, sweet chilli sauce and nam pla together and taste, adding a little more of any of the ingredients you fancy. Pour over the cucumber. Stir in the coriander leaves just before serving.

- No time? Missing a couple of ingredients? Just serve them with sweet chilli sauce.

WITH FRESH TOMATO SALSA
Serves 2

Only really worth making in the summer when tomatoes are ripe – and cheap.

4-5 ripe tomatoes (or a small pack of cherry tomatoes)
$1/2$ a small onion or $1/4$ medium onion, finely chopped
1 mild green chilli, cut lengthways, seeds removed and finely chopped
Juice of 1 lime
1 heaped tbsp chopped fresh coriander
Salt

Remove the tomato skins by making a small cut in the top of each tomato, placing them in a bowl and pouring boiling water over them. After a minute drain off the water and plunge them into cold water. The skins should come away easily. Finely chop the tomato flesh and seeds and place in a bowl with the chopped onion, chilli and lime juice. Season with salt and stir in the fresh coriander.

WITH GARLIC MAYO AND BUTTERED SPINACH Serves 2

Don't hesitate to use frozen spinach for this dish. It's much better value and quicker to prepare than the fresh stuff.

350g frozen leaf spinach (not chopped spinach which is just like baby food)
A small slice of butter (about 15g)
Salt, freshly ground black pepper and lemon juice
2-3 heaped tbsp garlic-flavoured mayonnaise (or plain mayonnaise mixed with either a clove of garlic, peeled and crushed or 1 tsp garlic paste)

Defrost the spinach in the microwave with 1 tablespoon of water or heat gently in a small pan with a lid on. When it's completely thawed, strain it in a sieve then return it to the pan with the butter and cook over a low heat till the butter has melted. Season with salt and pepper – and a little nutmeg if you've got it. Mix the mayonnaise with the crushed garlic or garlic paste and season with salt, pepper and a squeeze of lemon juice. Serve the fish fingers with a good dollop of the mayo and a portion of buttered spinach on the side.

CHICKEN BRUSCHETTA

Serves 1

Even breaded chicken and turkey steaks – always on special offer – can be given a healthy spin.

3 medium-sized ripe tomatoes
Salt and freshly ground black pepper
Squeeze of lemon juice
4-5 fresh basil leaves or a couple of sprigs of fresh parsley
2 tbsp olive oil
1 large or 2 small breaded chicken or turkey fillets

Skin the tomatoes as described in the Tomato Salsa recipe (*see* opposite). Chop them roughly and season with salt and pepper. Tear the basil leaves into small pieces or, if using parsley, chop and mix with the tomato. Pour over a teaspoon of olive oil. Heat a frying pan and add the remaining oil then cook the chicken fillet(s) until crisp and brown (about 5-6 minutes) turning them a couple of times. Top with the chopped tomato.

The Italian way of cooking scallopini or escalopes – wafer thin slices of meat – is perfectly suited to cooking on the run.

WITH LEMON, CAPERS AND PARSLEY Serves 2

2 large turkey escalopes
1 tbsp plain flour, seasoned with salt and pepper
2 tbsp olive oil
Juice of 1 lemon (about 3 tbsp)
1 tbsp capers, rinsed and roughly chopped
2 tbsp chopped fresh parsley
25g butter, cut into cubes

Lay a sheet of greaseproof paper or cling film over the the escalopes and bash them with a rolling pin or an empty wine bottle to make them thinner (obviously don't bash too hard if you're using a bottle). Put the seasoned flour in a shallow bowl and dip the escalope into the flour, covering both sides. Heat a frying pan over a moderate heat, and once it's hot add the oil. Lower the escalope into the pan and cook for about 2 minutes each side until lightly browned. Remove from the pan. Add the lemon juice, capers and parsley and bubble up in the pan. Add the butter and check the seasoning.

Pour over the escalopes. This goes really well with green beans and new potatoes.

• Capers are a tasty ingredient for zipping up pasta sauces and pizza toppings. To make a really good home-made tartare sauce combine 1 tbsp rinsed, chopped capers with 2 large dollops of mayo and 1 pickled cucumber or 5-6 gherkins, finely chopped. Add a little of the liquid from the pickled cucumber jar to thin the sauce.
• If the budget won't stretch to capers add a crushed clove of garlic instead.

SICILIAN STYLE Serves 1

This recipe is traditionally made with dry Marsala but medium dry Spanish Montilla (a very similar product to sherry) is a cheaper alternative. British 'sherry' would do at a pinch.

1 large turkey escalope
1 tbsp plain flour, seasoned with salt and pepper
1 small glass (about 75ml) medium dry Montilla or British medium 'sherry'
1/2 tsp dried thyme or 1/2 tsp fresh thyme leaves (optional)
2 tbsp olive oil
A small chunk of butter (about 15g)
1 tsp fresh or Jif lemon juice
Salt and pepper

Follow the first scallopini recipe (opposite page) up to the point where you've fried both sides of the escalopes. Add the Montilla and thyme if using and let the Montilla bubble up for a few seconds. Remove the escalope from the pan then continue to cook the sauce until it has reduced by half.

Add the butter and lemon juice, season with salt and pepper then pour the sauce over the escalope. This goes well with ribbon pasta like tagliatelle or fettucine or new potatoes and spinach.

FRENCH-STYLE WITH CREAM AND MUSHROOMS Serves 2

A bit indulgent but at least the mushrooms are healthy. And cream is really cheap....

2 large turkey escalopes
1 tbsp flour, seasoned with salt and pepper
2 tbsp olive oil
A good slice of butter (about 25g)
125g button mushrooms, rinsed clean and sliced
4 tbsp white wine or dry cider (drinkable not vinegary)
4 tbsp double cream
Salt, pepper and lemon juice to taste

Follow the first scallopini recipe (opposite page), using half the oil and butter, up to the point where you've fried both sides of the escalopes. Remove the escalopes and up the heat, add the remaining oil and butter to the pan and stir-fry the mushrooms for 4-5 minutes until brown. Pour in the white wine, stir it round the pan to get the stuck-on meaty bits off then take the pan off the heat and stir in the cream. Put the pan back on a low heat for a minute to let the cream warm through then season with salt, pepper and about a teaspoon of lemon juice. Pour over the escalopes. This goes well with new or boiled potatoes.

- If you have any uncooked mushrooms leftover you can make a simple salad by just slicing them and dressing them with the Italian-Style Oil, Lemon and Parsley Dressing (see p56).

KEBDA Serves 2

If you can overcome your squeamishness about liver this is a fantastic recipe – popular in one form or another throughout the middle east and North Africa. The pepper salad, which should be made first, is a great accompaniment but shop around for a good deal on peppers – they can be pricey out of season (through the winter).

250-300g lamb's liver
2 tsp flour
2 tsp ground cumin (or 2 tsp cumin seeds, crushed with a mortar and pestle)
1 tsp paprika
   (or 1/2 tsp if it's hot paprika)
1/4 tsp salt
2 tbsp oil
2 tbsp lemon juice
   (about 1/2 a lemon)
2 heaped tsp plain, unsweetened yoghurt
2 tbsp roughly chopped coriander

Remove any tubes from the liver (sorry, this is the unappealing bit) and cut into slices, if it's not already sliced. Mix the flour, cumin, paprika and salt in a shallow dish and dip the liver in it making sure each bit is thoroughly coated. Heat a large frying pan over a medium heat and add the oil. When the oil is hot lay the slices of liver in the pan. Cook for about 1 minute till you see blood appear on the surface (again, sorry, but if you've got this far I'm sure you're robust enough to cope with it) then turn over and cook the other side for another minute or two. Divide the liver between two plates and add the lemon juice to the pan. Let it bubble up and pour it over the liver. Top with a spoonful of yoghurt and some chopped coriander. Accompany with the warm pepper salad that follows.

WARM PEPPER SALAD

V Ve Serves 2

2 red peppers
2 cloves of garlic
2 tbsp olive oil
Salt and pepper

Quarter the peppers and cut away the stalk and all the white pith inside. Peel the garlic and cut into thin slices. Heat a frying pan or wok, add the oil and stir-fry the peppers over a medium heat until beginning to soften. Turn the heat right down and chuck in the garlic. Cook stirring occasionally until the peppers are completely soft. Season and set aside for 10 minutes or so.

TERIYAKI STEAK

Serves 1

*Steak might seem like a bit of a luxury for this section but if you buy basic frying steak it costs very little and only takes a moment to cook. For best value buy it from a butcher or the butcher's counter of a supermarket who will sell it in small amounts.
(It also goes by the name 'minute steak' or ask for a couple of thin slices of top rump.)*

1 thin slice of frying steak (about 125g)
2 tbsp Japanese teriyaki marinade, available in all good supermarkets
1 small clove of garlic, peeled and crushed
A small chunk of fresh ginger, grated or 1/4 tsp ginger paste (optional)
2 spring onions
1 tbsp oil

Trim any fat off the steak, lay it on a chopping board and give it a good bash with a rolling pin (or, even better, a meat tenderiser). Place it in a shallow bowl and pour over the teriyaki marinade. Leave it for 15 minutes or longer if possible, turning it over from time to time. Cut the roots and half the green tops off the spring onions, discard, cut the onions into four lengthways and then across into two. Take the steak out of the marinade and pat dry with kitchen towel. Heat a frying pan until quite hot, add the oil, swirl around the pan then add the steak. Cook for 1 minute on each side then remove from the pan. Chuck in the spring onions, garlic and ginger and stir-fry until just cooked (about a minute). Pour the marinade and an equal amount of water into the pan, let it bubble up and pour over the steak. It would go well with noodles and a salad topped with the Asian-Style Low-Fat Dressing (*see* p56).

• You can also use teriyaki sauce to marinade chicken or salmon.

All student cookbooks devote a couple of pages to baked potatoes but at the risk of provoking a sackful of hate mail I think they're overrated. Granted they're cheap but they're not quick. A good baked potato takes an hour to an hour and a quarter to cook – 15 minutes to heat the oven – 45-60 minutes to cook – so they're certainly not worth doing just for one. You can of course cook them quicker in a microwave but that makes them disgustingly soggy. A compromise is to cook them for half the recommended time in the microwave then finish them off in the oven so at least you'll get a crispy skin. If you want to speed the process up buy medium sized potatoes. Those gigantic footballs of spuds they sell for baking take an age.

For hardened baked potato addicts for whom none of that matters....

Six steps to a perfect baked potato

- Prick the skin with a fork in several places beforehand to ensure it doesn't burst.
- Rub a little oil into the skin to make it crisp.
- Cook in a hot oven – at least 200°C/400°F/Gas 6 – for 45 minutes to an hour.
- To speed up the cooking time impale the potatoes on a baked potato spike or stick a metal skewer through the middle.
- Make sure all your potatoes are roughly the same size so they cook in the same time.
- Cut a cross in the centre of each baked potato as you take it out of the oven then, protecting your hands with oven gloves, squeeze the sides of the potato so it opens up at the top. This lets the steam escape and makes the potato fluffier.

Some things you might not have thought to put in a baked potato

- Soft garlic and herb cheese
- Fried chorizo, peppers and onions – or just fried peppers and onions.
- Sour cream and Danish 'caviar' (lumpfish roe).
- Fresh pesto (available from the chill counter).
- Flash-fried steak strips with a dollop of creamed horseradish.
- Marmalade and kippers... just kidding (actually, boil-in-the-bag kippers wouldn't be bad).

Sweet baked potatoes

Much more interesting! Find them at most supermarkets but much more cheaply at markets or Caribbean stores. Treat them just like ordinary potatoes – scrub them clean, rub them with a little oil and roast them at 200°C/400°F/Gas 6 for about 45-50 minutes. Their bright orange colour and sweet flavour makes them a good accompaniment for chilli beans or a spicy vegetable stew.

GOOEY CHEESE FONDUE POTATOES ✿

Serves 1 (or more)

If it's potatoes that get you going rather than the fact they're baked just try this amazingly easy recipe.

For each person you will need

150g new potatoes or 2 medium
  potatoes or 1 large potato,
  scrubbed and cut into large
  chunks (leave the skins on
  for extra flavour, healthier too)
Salt and freshly ground black
  pepper
A good chunk (60-75g) Cheddar
  cheese
1 level tsp plain flour
2-3 tbsp milk
2 slices of onion, finely chopped
  (optional)

Bring a pan of water to the boil (use a kettle to boil the water – it's quicker). Add salt and the potatoes and cook for about 15 minutes until you can easily stick the point of a knife into them. Drain. Meanwhile grate the cheese and put it in another saucepan. Mix in the flour and the milk and heat very gently until it turns into a smooth sauce (about 2-3 minutes). Season with salt and pepper and a little finely chopped onion, if you want to zip it up a bit. Pour the cheese sauce over the potatoes. If you want to assuage your guilt have a salad with it.

(*See also* **MASH** and **HASH**, pp110-113.)

Bread is such a staple that it's easy to go onto automatic pilot in the supermarket and reach for the cheapest sliced loaf you can get your hands on.

Of course there are moments (see **LATE NIGHT FUEL**) when nothing but a soggy bacon sarnie will do but in general cheap bread just isn't that filling or satisfying. It's not that there isn't an alternative. Baguettes, pitta bread, naan and ciabatta are all more interesting bases for sandwiches and usually one or other will be on special offer. And good bread that's reduced (because it's reached its sell-by date) makes great toast.

STUFFED PITTA BREADS WITH FELAFEL, SALAD AND GARLICKY YOGHURT DRESSING ☘ Serves 2-3

For the dressing
2 large spoonfuls very low-fat yoghurt
1 small or 1/2 large clove of garlic, peeled and crushed
A pinch of cumin
Salt

2 tbsp oil
200g pack felafel
3 plain or wholewheat pitta breads
1/2 an onion, peeled and thinly sliced
2 medium tomatoes, thinly sliced or a chunk of cucumber
Some iceberg lettuce leaves or other salad leaves

To make the dressing, combine the yoghurt with the crushed garlic and cumin. Season with salt. Heat the oil in a frying pan and fry the felafel for about 5 minutes, turning them regularly so they cook evenly.

Turn them onto a plate and squash them slightly with the back of a fork. Heat the pitta breads under a grill or pop them in a toaster on a low setting. (You want them warm and puffy rather than hard). Cut them in half, open up each half and stuff with the felafel, onion, slices of tomato, a few lettuce leaves and spoon over the yoghurt dressing.

Other fillings for pitta breads
- Make as above replacing the felafel with the chickpeas from the Egyptian-Style Eggs with Chickpeas recipe (see p53) or leftover Black Bean Chilli (see p122).
- Taramasalata and sliced cucumber.
- Greekish Salad (see p59).
- Any leftover grilled or barbecued veg with hummus.

'HERO' SANDWICHES WITH SALAMI, CHEESE AND PICKLES Serves 2

Hero sandwiches are a classic American invention, the idea being to cram in heroic amounts of filling.

1 ready-to-bake ciabatta
  or a small baguette
1/2 a pack of Jarlsberg,
  Emmental or Cheddar
  (about 125g)
A large pickled cucumber
  or some gherkins
Soft or spreadable butter
  or other spread
1 tsp Dijon mustard
1 pack salami, garlic sausage or
  mortadella – whatever's cheap
Ground black pepper
1 tbsp mayonnaise

Cut the ciabatta vertically in half then split each half lengthways. Heat a grill and toast each piece on the outside (you don't need to do this with a fresh baguette). Cool for a couple of minutes while you slice the cheese and the gherkins.

Spread each cut surface lightly with butter or butter substitute. Spread the two bases with mustard then top with slices of salami, cheese and pickled cucumber or gherkins. Season with freshly ground black pepper, spread the cut side of the other 2 pieces of ciabatta with mayo then press down firmly on top.

Other things to put in a baguette
- Ham and Dijon mustard.
- Pâté and pickled cucumber.
- Brie and cranberry sauce.

... or a ciabatta
- Warm pepper salad (*see* p68) or cold roast peppers, goats cheese or other soft cheese and rocket, watercress or other dark green salad leaves.
- Slices of cold chicken, avocado and crispy bacon with a spoonful of French mustard dressing. Or just a plain BLT – bacon, lettuce and tomato.

COTTAGE CHEESE, GARLIC AND CORIANDER NAAN 🍁
Serves 1

If you're a coriander fan this is for you. Even if you don't normally like cottage cheese.

1/2 a large or 1 medium or 2
  small garlic and coriander naan
2 tsp fresh coriander paste
  (cheapest in an Asian grocer)
  or 1 heaped tbsp finely
  chopped coriander leaves
2 tbsp cottage cheese

Cut the naan if necessary to fit in a toaster or toast each side under a grill until brown but not brittle. Split the pieces open and allow to cool for a minute. Spread the base with the coriander paste and spoon over the cottage cheese. Press the top half down and eat, preferably while the bread is still warm.

THE BEST EVER CHEESE ON TOAST 🍁

Serves 1

This is the best way I've found of making cheese on toast as the toast doesn't burn or go soggy like it does in a microwave. You can of course leave out the chilli and onions if you're a purist.

A good chunk (75-100g)
   Cheddar or Lancashire cheese
1 tsp flour
1-2 mild green chillies
1 tbsp finely chopped onion or
   a spring onion, trimmed and
   finely sliced (optional)
1-2 tbsp milk (2 if you use more
   cheese)
A couple of thick slices of
   bread, preferably wholemeal
A little hot chilli sauce or a pinch
   of chilli powder or cayenne
   pepper

Grate the cheese, put it into a small saucepan, add the flour and blend together. Cut the chillies in half lengthways and scrape out the seeds. Add the chopped onion if using and 2 tablespoons of milk. Heat gently, stirring while you make the toast. As soon as the cheese mixture is smooth pour over the toast and shake over a little chilli sauce.

• Instead of chilli and onion you could add 1 tsp mustard or ½ tsp Worcestershire Sauce to the melted cheese.

ITALIAN BREAD 'PIZZA'
🍁 Serves 2

Ciabatta is a better base than a baguette for a French bread pizza but if you can't afford it a baguette will do fine.

½ a ready to bake ciabatta
   or a small baguette
4-5 tbsp The Easiest Ever Pasta
   Sauce (see p44) or other
   tomato based pasta sauce
   or 2 sliced, ripe tomatoes
½ tsp oregano or herbes de
   Provence
½ a pack (about 125g) grated
   Cheddar, Lancashire or other
   medium to strong English
   cheese
Freshly ground black pepper

Cut the piece of ciabatta or baguette lengthways into two. (If using a baguette press each half down firmly with the heel of your hand to make a flat surface.) Toast lightly on both sides. Spread the cut side with the pasta sauce or tomatoes, sprinkle over the oregano then cover with slices of cheese. Put back under a hot grill and grill for about 2-3 minutes until the cheese has melted. Grind over some black pepper.

- You could add a layer of salami if you want to make this more substantial.
- For a really ritzy version see **FEASTS**.

GARLIC MUSHROOMS ON TOAST 🍁 Serves 2

One of the simplest, most delicious ways to eat mushrooms.

A small pack (about 250g) button mushrooms
1 tbsp olive oil
A small chunk of butter (about 15g)
1 small clove garlic, crushed or finely chopped or $1/2$ tsp fresh garlic paste
1 tbsp double cream or crème fraîche (optional)
Salt and pepper
Squeeze of lemon juice (optional)

Rinse the mushrooms under cold water, removing any dirt and slice roughly. Heat a small frying pan over a moderate heat, add the oil, then the butter. Once the butter melts tip in the mushrooms and stir them around. Add the garlic then continue to cook for 4-5 minutes until browned. Stir in the cream if using and season with salt and pepper and a little lemon juice if you've added cream. Serve on hot buttered toast.

- Try this with Mozzarella. Leave out the cream, spoon the mushrooms on toast, cover with thin slices of Mozzarella or Brie and place the toast under a hot grill till the cheese melts.

SARDINE TARTINES
Serves 1

Sardines are a trusty friend when funds are severely depleted.

1 small can of sardines
1 thick slice of wholemeal bread
1 clove of garlic, peeled and cut in half
1 tsp fresh or Jif lemon juice
1 tbsp finely chopped fresh parsley
Black pepper

Drain the oil or brine from the can. Cut each sardine in half lengthways, split it open and remove the backbone. Toast the bread and rub with the cut garlic. Arrange the sardines on top of the toast and scatter over the parsley. Squeeze over the lemon and grind some black pepper. Good with a green salad (see p57).

One of the reasons I suspect we don't eat as much fruit as we should do is that it's hard to get fruit that's really ripe, particularly if you haven't got much to spend on it. A major reason is that supermarkets insist on selling fruit like strawberries and peaches out of season so they're never going to be anything but rock hard.

The answer is to make fruit more of a treat, either by cooking it (a good bet in winter) and/or adding a bit of sugar, honey or something creamy (but not necessarily fattening) to it like yoghurt and low-fat fromage frais. And don't turn up your nose at tinned fruit.

BROWN SUGAR BANANAS 🍁 Serves 2

Not that most of us need any encouragement to eat bananas but here's something to do with them if they're not quite ripe (i.e. still greenish rather than smothered in black spots).

2 medium not too ripe bananas
25g soft butter
1 heaped tbsp soft brown sugar
Juice of half a lime or half an
   orange

Peel and thinly slice the banana. Heat a frying pan until hot then add the butter When it stops foaming tip in the banana and stir-fry for a minute. Sprinkle over the sugar, carry on stirring until the sugar starts to look like hardening then pour in the lime or orange juice. As soon as the sizzling dies down tip the bananas and sauce in a bowl. Serve with something rich and creamy like Greek yoghurt, double cream or vanilla ice cream. (Rinse the pan immediately under hot water or you'll never get it clean.)

- You could include a few chopped nuts when you add the banana for extra crunch.

PAN-FRIED APPLE WITH HONEY, LEMON AND GINGER 🍁🍁 Serves 1

Obviously leave out the ginger if you don't like ginger. It still tastes good.

1 good quality crisp eating apple
   (such as Blenheim or Cox)
A small chunk of butter
   (about 15g)
A little grated fresh ginger or
   1/4 tsp ginger paste or 1/4 tsp
   ground ginger
1 tbsp of runny honey
1 tbsp of lemon juice

Cut the apple into quarters, core and cut each quarter lenthways into three. Heat a small frying pan then add the butter. Just as it starts foaming throw in the apple pieces, coat them in butter then quickly lay them out in a single layer.

Cook for about two minutes on each side until lightly browned then sprinkle over the ginger. Spoon over the honey and just as it starts to caramelise (about 30 seconds) add the lemon juice. Bubble up for a minute until the juices are reduced then tip the mixture into a bowl. Spoon over some plain or soy yoghurt and serve.

- You could also make this with pears or peaches.

WARM APPLE AND CINNAMON COMPOTE
Serves 2

Classic comfort food. But, unusually, quite healthy too. Use Bramley apples or they won't break down into a soft goo.

2 large Bramley apples
2 tbsp caster or granulated sugar
A pinch (about 1/4 tsp) cinnamon

Quarter the apples, remove the core, peel and cut into chunky slices. (Don't worry if they start to go brown while you're doing this.) Put the pieces into a saucepan with the sugar, cinnamon and 3 tablespoons of water and cover with a lid or a piece of foil. Put the pan over a moderate heat and cook, shaking the pan occasionally until the apples fluff up and begin to disintegrate (about 7-10 minutes). Take off the heat and beat with a wooden spoon till smooth (or leave them chunky if you prefer). Serve straightaway with cream or custard or cold with yoghurt (very good with muesli).

There are lots of other good things to do with fruit.

If you're anywhere near a market lookout for bargains on some of the following...

- Chunks of ripe mango with lime juice squeezed over them.
- Thick slices of fresh pineapple, sprinkled with sugar and grilled.
- Strawberries, sliced and sprinkled with sugar with low-fat fromage frais.
- Ripe peaches or apricots with plain yoghurt, honey and chopped walnuts.
- A big slice of honeydew melon and some wafer-thin smoked ham.
- A chunk of Brie and some grapes or cherries.
- Sliced kiwifruit and cottage cheese.
- A pear, some crumbled Danish Blue cheese and a green salad.
- *See also* Roughie recipes, p81.

Assuming you've had the strength of will to pass the chippy, hamburger stand and local Indian on your way home – or were simply too late for them – here's how to bring a bit of international sophistication to your late-night eating without exerting yourself unduly.

PEA AND PIE FLOATERS Serves 2

Before the days when they were as likely to grab a Pad Thai as a pie this was classic Aussie post-pub grub. You can obviously double or treble it for larger numbers.

2 individual steak and kidney
   or minced beef pies
1 small tin of mushy peas
1 portion Amazing Marmite
   Gravy (see below)

Heat the oven to about 190C/Gas 5 or whatever temperature is recommended on the pack. Put the pies on a baking tray and cook for about 20 minutes. Heat the mushy peas in a pan or the microwave with a tablespoon or two of water. Ladle the peas into soup bowls, plonk a pie in the middle then pour gravy around it. Eat with a spoon.

❤ For a veggie version use ½ a pack of frozen Yorkshire puddings.

AMAZING MARMITE GRAVY Ⓥ Ⓥ

This may sound wildly unlikely but believe me it works. And it's so much better than gravy granules....

1 tbsp (15g) soft butter
1 tbsp plain flour
1 tsp Marmite

Measure out 225ml (about a mugful) of boiling water and dissolve the Marmite in it. Melt the butter gently in a saucepan and stir in the flour. Cook over a low heat for a minute then add the Marmite stock, stirring continously. Bring back to the boil and simmer till ready to use.

LOCO MOCO Serves 2

To be honest I've only included this because of the great name. Apparently it's Hawaii's favourite fast food which doesn't say a lot for Hawaiin cuisine. But if you make it with decent burgers and serve it with a good slosh of chilli sauce it's strangely satisfying. Or at least would be at around 3 a.m. in the morning.

225ml Amazing Marmite Gravy
   (see opposite page)
2 fresh or frozen quarter-pounder
   beefburgers or veggie burgers
1 tbsp oil
1 250g packet Express rice
   (like Uncle Bens) or a small
   packet of microwaveable rice
2 eggs

Make up the gravy as described and leave to simmer. Heat the oil in a frying pan and fry the beefburgers until both sides are well browned. Remove from the pan. Microwave or steam the rice. Fry the eggs until the white has set but the yolk is still runny.

Make a mound of the rice on each plate, top with a burger, pour over half the gravy then top with a fried egg. Serve with medium or hot pepper sauce (my preference), tomato ketchup or HP or another brown sauce.

NACHOS 🍁 Serves 4

This Tex Mex snack is much healthier without the gloopy cheese sauce that usually gets served with it. You can of course buy ready-grated cheese but it'll cost you.

1 small pack (175-200g)
   Cheddar or any hard regional
   British cheese such as Double
   Gloucester, Red Leicester,
   Caerphilly or Wensleydale
1/2 a jar of jalapeno peppers or
   chilli sauce
1 200g pack lightly salted tortilla
   chips

Grate the cheese coarsely. Drain the peppers and chop roughly. Put about a quarter of the tortilla chips in a bowl, sprinkle over a quarter of the cheese and microwave for a minute. Scatter over 1/4 of the peppers or pour over a little chilli sauce. Repeat with the rest of the tortillas and cheese. (It's better microwaving it bowl by bowl so you don't have to cook it too long)

- At any other time of day rustle up some Fresh Tomato Salsa (see p64) instead of the jalapenos.

Some slightly healthier late-night fuel options
- Scrambled Eggs (see p54).
- Egg-Fried Rice (see p116).
- A couple of hardboiled eggs (see p52).
- Best Ever Cheese on Toast (see p74).
- Microwaved porridge.
- A tin of rice pudding.
- Jelly (see p163).

FEELING ROUGH, FEELING STRESSED

Whether it's self-inflicted or you've succumbed to a bug there are times when you need to give your system a break and recharge your batteries. The easiest way to do this is by following a liquid – or near liquid – diet for 24 hours. And I don't mean booze.

Soup is the obvious starting point (*see* pp86-91) but if you're feeling under par you're not going to want to start making it from scratch. Most instant soups are pretty disgusting – you'd actually be better to make a simple broth with a decent chicken stock cube (kosher ones such as Telma are best) or vegetable bouillon powder. If you find it bland you can infuse the hot broth for 5 minutes with flavourings such as lime leaf, ginger and garlic. Instant miso soup is also really comforting and filling but improved with a finely sliced spring onion floated in it.

REAL THAI CUP-A-SOUP 🌿 🌿

Serves 1

To get the full-on Thai flavour you need as many as possible of these ingredients, especially the lime leaf, ginger and chilli but it's still going to taste good if you just use ginger, garlic, fish sauce and lime.

300ml boiling stock made with 1 tsp vegetable bouillon powder or $1/3$-$1/2$ chicken stock cube
2 fine slices of fresh ginger or galangal
2 fine slices of garlic
1 lime leaf
1 stalk of lemongrass, halved and roughly crushed or $1/2$ tsp lemongrass paste
1-2 stalks of coriander, halved and roughly crushed
A deseeded and finely chopped chilli
A squeeze of lime juice

Make up the stock in a jug or saucepan and add all the other ingredients. Cover the jug or pan and leave for 5 minutes. Strain into a mug (use a sieve or tea strainer) and add a small squeeze of lime juice or a couple of drops of chilli sauce if you think it needs it.

• If the problem is a sore throat or a cold, a mug of fresh lemon juice (about 3 tbsp) and 1-2 tsp honey topped up with boiling water is very soothing. A good vitamin C boost too.

If you're feeling a bit brighter you could move on to a roughie. Roughie? Roughies are what to make when you fancy a smoothie but haven't got a blender... or if you have but can't be bothered to wash it up.

BANANA, YOGHURT AND HONEY ROUGHIE
Serves 1

1 ripe banana
1 large dollop plain, low-fat yoghurt
A little runny honey to sweeten
A handful of muesli (optional)

Peel and slice the banana into a bowl and mash thoroughly with a fork. Add the yoghurt and a little honey to taste (I suggest about 1/2 a teaspoon). Mash again. That's it. If you want a bit more crunch add a handful of muesli.

RASPBERRY RIPPLE ROUGHIE
Serves 1

1/2 small punnet of raspberries or around 60g of frozen raspberries, thawed
1/2-1 tsp caster sugar
2 tablespoons of plain, low-fat yoghurt

Put the raspberries in a bowl and mash thoroughly. Sweeten to taste with sugar. Half-stir in the yoghurt leaving it streaky (yes, I know you're only making it for yourself but it still looks more appealing than making it bright pink). Add a handful of muesli as above if you fancy it.

• You can basically make a roughie with any squishable, ripe fruit – strawberries, mangoes and peaches would all be good. Or use canned fruit.

Light Eating

Once you do start eating proper meals again stick to light, non-fatty foods. Eggs are perfect, though boil or scramble rather than fry them. Fish is more digestible than meat especially if microwaved or steamed (*see* pp62-63), and eat as much fresh fruit and raw or plainly cooked veg as you can (like the Morrocan Spiced Carrot Salad, *see* p57). Pasta is fine if you avoid rich creamy or cheesy sauces and if you're recovering from a bout of gastro-enteritis a simple dish of boiled rice and peas won't tax the system too much. Nor will a few pieces of vegetarian sushi.

EGGIES IN A CUP ❦

Serves 1

This is real baby food but if you feel really bad there's nothing like it. Best made with a proper old-fashioned white loaf but sliced bread will do.

1 thick slice of fresh white bread
   with the crusts cut off
1-2 eggs
1-2 tsp soft butter
Salt and pepper

Crumble the bread into a large cup. Boil the eggs in boiling water for $3^1/_2$-4 minutes depending on whether they're medium or large. Break the top off the eggs, then scoop them into the cup, add the butter and mash up with the breadcrumbs. Season with a little salt and pepper.

Preventing that hangover...

You know this already I'm sure but you shouldn't drink on an empty stomach. Even a glass of milk will stop the alcohol going straight into your bloodstream and making you drunk. Better still would be a glass of milk and a banana or a couple of pieces of toast. Once you do start drinking dilute the effect by having regular glasses of water – one for every drink you have. Down a couple more before you go to bed. And if you want to avoid a splitting headache don't mix wine and spirits.

Good eating habits tend to go out of the window during exam time, essay deadlines or other periods of stress, but you don't actually do yourself any favours if you starve your body – or brain – of essential nutrients. Staying up all night fuelled by caffeine may make you feel like you're on top of things but a Horlicks or herbal tea-induced night's sleep would make you function a lot better.

Keep yourself going with nourishing snacks, a bowl of cereal, a health bar, a yoghurt, a piece of fruit. This is the sort of time ready-meals do come in handy, so be prepared to overspend your budget if necessary to save yourself the bother of having to think about meals. Drink plenty of water too.

Before an exam try and eat something even if you're sick with nerves – a bowl of cereal, some fruit and yoghurt if it's first thing, a bowl of soup and a sandwich or a plate of pasta before an afternoon exam. Or a smoothie if you can't face anything solid.

If you're having trouble sleeping stick to herbal teas such as camomile and lemon verbena or milky drinks rather than coffee.

PRE-EXAM SMOOTHIE
🅥 Serves 1

If you haven't got a blender, food processor or a hand-held blender, use the roughie technique (see p81), mashing the banana as smoothly as you can.

125ml good quality orange juice (preferably the freshly squeezed type)
1 medium ripe banana
2 large spoonfuls of yoghurt
1 tsp runny honey

Peel and slice the banana and put in the blender or food processor with the yoghurt and honey. Whizz until smooth then add the orange juice and whizz again. Pour into a large glass. Remember to clean blender once exam is over.

FAVOURITES

If you're sharing a house where you take turns to cook it makes sense to make dishes that most of you will like. These can be family favourites like spaghetti bolognese or macaroni cheese or simply recipes that you're happy to keep going back to because they're cheap and delicious.

The best way to gain confidence in your cooking is to get to grips with a particular type of dish – soups, say, or stew – so that you get to the stage where you can make it without even looking at the recipe. These can be your specialities – the dishes you make when it's your turn to cook.

Some of these recipes need to be cooked in the oven so they'll take a bit longer than the recipes in the first section. That doesn't mean you have to stand slavishly over the cooker. Just get things going then go off and do something else. If you haven't got money you need patience....

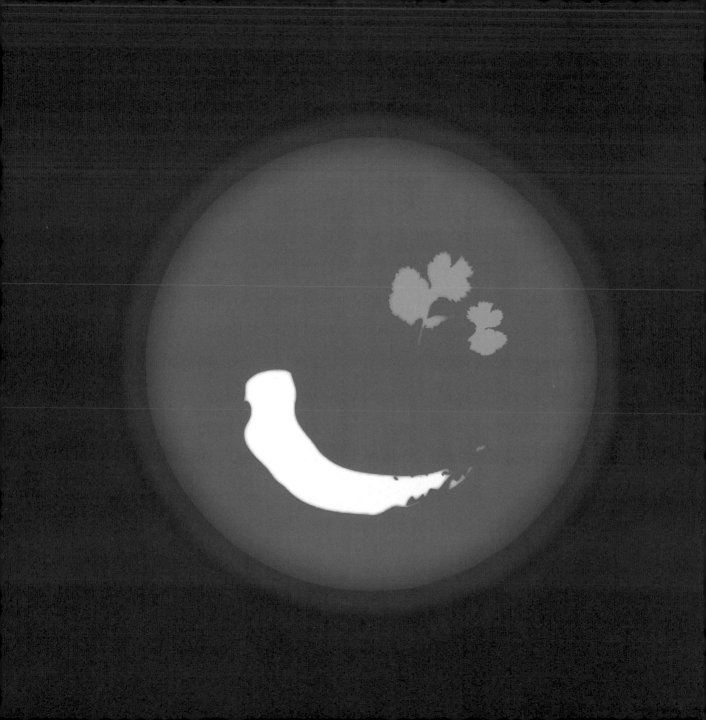

In terms of comfort food, soup has to be up there along with chocolate and mashed potato. Especially if you've made it yourself. It's also one of the most economical things to cook – you can make soup with virtually anything.

Chunky soups are a good place to start because you don't even have to purée them. You just cook your vegetables in a bit of butter or oil to soften them, add stock or water and wait for them to cook. That's it.

CHUNKY POTATO, ONION AND GARLIC SOUP V Ve Serves 2-4

This is probably the cheapest recipe in the book. The key is the long slow cooking which gives the onions a really sweet flavour.

4 tbsp olive oil or 2 tbsp oil and a good chunk of butter (about 25g)
2 large onions, halved, peeled and cut into thin slices
1 large clove of garlic, peeled and finely chopped or crushed
1 large potato, peeled, quartered and cut into thin slices
1/2 tsp of dried thyme and/or a couple of bay leaves
1 litre of vegetable stock made with 1 tbsp of Marigold vegetable bouillon powder or a stock cube
A good handful of parsley, stalks removed and leaves roughly chopped or a handful of finely shredded green cabbage or spring greens
Salt and pepper

Heat the oil in a large pan. Add the butter then chuck in the onions and garlic. Turn them thoroughly in the butter and oil then turn the heat down and put a lid or some foil over the pan. Cook, stirring occasionally for about 25 minutes until the onions are really soft and sweet. Add the potato and herbs to the pan, pour in the stock and bring to the boil. Simmer uncovered for another 20 minutes or so, adding the cabbage, if using, about 5 minutes before the cooking time is up. Check seasoning, adding salt and pepper to taste. Add the parsley if using, cook for a couple of minutes then serve up.

- You could make a quicker version by using 2-3 leeks instead of onions (*see* p31 for how to prepare leeks) which would take about 25 minutes in total. Leave out the garlic and sprinkle on a bit of grated Parmesan when you serve it.
- You could fry some chopped streaky bacon or bacon bits before you add the onions.

CHUNKY ITALIAN VEGETABLE SOUP 🍁

Serves 6

Obviously it's the vegetables that are chunky not the Italians. This is a formula you can vary endlessly depending on what veg are cheap and in season. It also reheats well if you want to leave some for the next day.

3 tbsp olive oil
2 medium onions, peeled and chopped
2 large cloves of garlic, crushed
2 sticks of celery, trimmed and sliced or a large carrot, peeled and chopped
1/2 400g can chopped tomatoes
1 litre vegetable stock made with 1 tbsp Marigold vegetable bouillon powder or a vegetable stock cube
2 medium courgettes (about 225g) trimmed and sliced into rounds
A handful of fresh green beans (about 125g) trimmed and quartered
410g can cannellini or borlotti beans
1/2 small green cabbage trimmed and finely shredded or 1/2 bag of ready-sliced greens or 3 tbsp chopped fresh parsley
2 tbsp red pesto
Salt and freshly ground black pepper
A little grated Parmesan

Heat the olive oil in a large saucepan or casserole and cook the onion and garlic over a low heat for about 5 minutes. Add the chopped celery or carrots, cook for a few minutes more then add the tomatoes and stock and bring to the boil. Lower the heat and simmer for about 15 minutes. Add the courgettes, green beans and cannellini beans and half the cabbage, if using, and cook for another 20 minutes or until all the vegetables are soft, adding the remaining cabbage or parsley and pesto about 10 minutes before the end of the cooking time. Season to taste with salt and pepper and serve with grated Parmesan.

A quick, no-chopping version

Forget the onion and the other veg. Cook the garlic in the oil for a minute, add 1/2 a can of tomatoes, smash them down a bit then add the stock and bring to the boil. Add a small packet (about 350g) of frozen vegetables, the cannellini beans and about 125g (a mugful) of small pasta shapes. Bring back to the boil and simmer for about 12-15 minutes till the vegetables are soft and the pasta is cooked. Add pesto and parsley as above.

To make soup velvety-smooth you obviously need a machine like a blender or food processor to whizz it in – or to whizz in it. Those hand-held blenders do a good job and are really cheap (see **KITCHEN KIT**). You also need to base your soup on a vegetable with a dominant flavour or colour, otherwise they can look like brown sludge. Swirling in a spoonful of yoghurt or cream at the end and sprinkling on some herbs will improve the appearance too.

CARROT AND CORIANDER SOUP

V **Ve** Makes 4 bowls

Carrots make really, really good soup.

2 tbsp sunflower oil or olive oil
1 medium onion, peeled and chopped or a couple of leeks, cleaned and roughly chopped
4 medium or 3 large carrots (about 350g) peeled and cut into rounds
1 medium potato, peeled and roughly chopped
A couple of sticks of celery (optional)
1 rounded tsp ground coriander or crushed coriander seeds
750ml vegetable stock made with 1 tbsp vegetable bouillon powder or a stock cube
Salt and pepper
Fresh coriander or parsley

Heat the oil in a large pan, add the onion, stir and cook over a low heat until soft (about 5 minutes). Add the carrots, potato and celery if using and stir again. Cover the pan with a lid or a piece of foil and cook very slowly for about 10 minutes. Stir in the ground or crushed coriander and pour in the stock. Bring to the boil and cook for about 20-25 minutes until the vegetables are soft. Blitz the soup with a hand held blender or put it through a blender or a food processor. Return to the pan and check the seasoning. Add salt and pepper to taste and a little extra water if you think it's too thick. Serve sprinkled with chopped fresh coriander or parsley.

• You can replace the potato with a small can of butterbeans.

PEA, BROCCOLI AND MINT SOUP 🍁

Makes 4 bowls

Eating your greens can sometimes seem a bit of a tyranny but one of the answers is to cunningly plunge them into a pea soup. The slight bitterness of the greens offsets the sweetness of the peas perfectly.

1 small head of broccoli (about 225-250g)
1 tbsp oil plus a small chunk of butter or 2 tbsp oil
1 small to medium onion, peeled and roughly chopped or 5-6 spring onions, trimmed and chopped
225g frozen peas
500ml stock made with 2 tsp vegetable bouillon powder or a chicken or vegetable stock cube
The leaves from a couple of sprigs of fresh mint or a small handful of fresh coriander or parsley
A small carton of single cream (optional)

Cut the florets of broccoli off the stalk then chop them roughly. Warm the oil in a large saucepan then add the butter and the onion, stir and cook over a gentle heat for about 5 minutes until soft. Add the peas and broccoli, pour in the stock and bring to the boil. Simmer until the vegetables are soft (about 5 minutes). Spoon the veg into a blender or food processor and whizz until smooth gradually adding the rest of the liquid (you may have to do this in two batches). Pour the soup back into the saucepan and season with salt and pepper to taste. Finely chop the herbs and stir in just before serving. You could also add a swirl of cream.

• You can cook the soup even more quickly if you microwave the broccoli first. Place the florets in a dish with a little boiling water, cover it with cling film, pierce the film, then cook on high for 3 minutes. Add to the soup with the peas and cook for about 2-3 minutes.

• Alternatively make the soup with a bunch of watercress or a handful of spinach instead of broccoli. Wash it, break off the tougher stems, chop it roughly and cook with the peas for about 2 minutes.

Clear soups are well suited to summer when you want light food – they're common in South-East Asia. The starting point should be a well-flavoured broth infusing spices and herbs in stock or water. Then it's simply a matter of adding some vegetables, herbs and meat if you like.

THAI STIR-FRY SOUP
Makes 4 bowls

I hesitated about including this soup because of the sheer number of ingredients but it's so good I couldn't leave it out. It's a bit galling admittedly to think that it would cost about 35p on the street in Bangkok but if you're into Thai food hopefully you'll have at least some of the ingredients already. And at least it's based on stir-fry veg which saves you a bit of chopping.

ONE:
THE CHICKEN VERSION

1 or 2 skinless chicken breasts

A small chunk (about 2 cm square) of galangal or fresh ginger peeled and sliced

A large clove of garlic, peeled and sliced

6 fresh or freeze-dried lime leaves finely sliced (if you use dried ones soak them in warm water for 5 minutes) or a couple of fine strips of lime peel

2 stalks of lemongrass, with the outer husk removed and halved or a tsp of lemongrass paste

A pack of stir-fry veg (the best you can afford – it's quite nice if it can include ingredients like baby corn and mange-tout), otherwise use a good handful of beansprouts and a handful of roughly chopped spinach or pak choi leaves

1-2 mild fresh red chillies (not those lethal little birds eye chillies, unless you're a chilli addict) deseeded and finely sliced

A good handful of fresh coriander leaves, roughly chopped or Thai basil (if you can get it)

1 tbsp nam pla (fish sauce) plus
   extra for serving (essential)
1 tbsp lime juice plus 1 lime,
   quartered
Hot chilli sauce for serving
   (optional)

Place the chicken in a saucepan
and pour over 700ml of water.
Bring slowly to the boil, spoon
off any scum then add the
galangal or ginger, garlic,
3 of the lime leaves and the
lemon grass. Simmer over a
very low heat so that the water
barely trembles for 20 minutes.
Remove the chicken and cut
into fine strips. Strain the stock,
return it to the pan and bring
it to a simmer. Add the stir-fry
vegetables, chillies and
remaining lime leaves and
cook for 3-4 minutes until the
vegetables are cooked. Then
add the chicken and heat for
another minute or two. Stir in
the coriander, nam pla and lime
juice, check the seasoning then
serve. Put additional nam pla,
chilli sauce and lime on the table
so everyone can add more if
they want.

- If you cook two chicken
  breasts you could save the
  remaining chicken for a salad.
- Instead of using chicken
  pieces you could make
  the soup from stock from
  a chicken carcass.
- If you want to make it more
  substantial add about 75g of
  rice noodles soaked in boiling
  water for 2 minutes when you
  add the chicken.

TWO: ❖
THE VEGGIE VERSION

Obviously leave out the chicken
and use vegetable stock made
with Marigold vegetable bouillon
powder instead, simmering it for
20 minutes with the garlic, lime
leaves etc as in the previous
recipe. If you like you can add
some sliced mushrooms
(about 125g) to the stir-fried
veg. Use light soy sauce instead
of nam pla.

A final word on soups...

Even top quality soups can be
improved. Tart up your shop-
bought tin or carton with a good
squeeze of lemon, a spoonful of
cream or yoghurt or a couple of
spoonfuls of chopped fresh
herbs. Also, thinning a soup
down with a little water will
make it taste more home-made.
Tomato-based soups are often
improved by adding a crushed
clove of garlic, a spoonful or
two of red pesto or a little mild
chilli powder.

Mince almost equals meat so far as many students are concerned but you need to take care these days you're not paying over the odds. Some mince, such as minced lamb or beef labelled extra-lean or extra-mature, is quite pricey.

SIMPLE SPAGHETTI BOLOGNESE Serves 4

Everybody seems to have their own recipe for spag bol, involving bacon, wine, mushrooms or some secret ingredient their mum always puts in it but the truth is the more stuff there is in it the more someone is likely to object to it. And you don't need it.

This simple recipe can also be used as the basis for others such as Chilli Con Carne (see p94). The initial frying may seem time-consuming but it gets rid of all the excess fat in the meat and really improves the flavour.

1 tbsp oil
500g mince
1 heaped tbsp concentrated tomato purée (you can buy it in tubes)
1-2 cloves of garlic, crushed or finely chopped or 1-2 tsp fresh garlic paste
1 tsp oregano or herbes de Provence
1 400g can chopped or whole tomatoes
Salt and pepper
500g spaghetti or other pasta shapes
Freshly grated Parmesan or other cheese to serve (optional)

Heat a frying pan over a moderately high heat for 2-3 minutes. Add the oil, swirl round the pan then add half the mince spreading it around the pan. Fry until beginning to brown then turn it over with a wooden spoon or spatula. Keep frying until all the mince is browned (about $1\frac{1}{2}$-2 minutes). Tip the pan away from you, scoop out the mince onto a large plate and discard the fat that has accumulated in the pan. Replace the pan on the hob and repeat with the remaining mince, discarding the fat again at the end. Turn down the heat a little and return all the meat to the pan without any further oil. Add the tomato paste, stir into the meat until it is well distributed, stirring it all the time. Add the garlic or garlic paste, the herbs and the tinned tomatoes (breaking them up with a fork if they are whole). Season with salt and pepper, bring to a simmer then turn the heat right down and leave to cook gently while you cook the spaghetti.

Bring a large pan of boiling water to the boil. Add salt then add the spaghetti pressing it down into the water as the ends soften until it is completely submerged. Stir it around with a large fork or spoon so the strands are separate, then continue to boil without stirring for the time recommended on the pack. Drain the spaghetti in a sieve or colander and divide between four plates. Top with the sauce and sprinkle with Parmesan or other grated cheese if you like it. (Alternatively you can tip the drained spaghetti in the sauce and mix it together.)

You could also add
- A small pack of bacon bits or 3-4 rashers of streaky bacon (fry after the mince and discard the fat).
- 5 or 6 thinly sliced washed button mushrooms.
- A handful of frozen peas.
- Some chopped fresh parsley.
- Half a small glass of red or white wine.

♣If you're vegetarian you can obviously make this – or any of the other mince recipes – with Quorn or soy mince.

! When discarding fat from the mince do not pour down the drain – it will block it. Instead pour into a cup, allow to solidify and then chuck it in the wastebin.

CHILLI CON CARNE

Serves 4-6

Once you've mastered the bolognese recipe chilli con carne is a doddle. You can easily expand the meal by adding an extra tin of beans.

Simple Spaghetti Bolognese
  sauce (*see* p92)
2-3 tsp mild chilli powder
1/2 tsp cumin (optional)
1-2 x 400g cans of red kidney
  beans
Fresh parsley or coriander
  (optional)
Sour cream (optional)

Make the sauce as described, adding 2 teaspoons of mild chilli powder and cumin, if using, when you add the garlic and herbs. Let the sauce simmer for 15 minutes then drain the kidney beans into a sieve and rinse under cold running water. Add the beans to the mince and heat through thoroughly for the flavours to amalgamate (about 10 minutes). Check seasoning, adding a little more chilli powder if needed. Serve on its own or with a dollop of sour cream and a few chopped herbs and a salad. Also good with baked potatoes.

• If you're making this for one or two you could split the Simple Spaghetti Bolognese recipe, serving half with spaghetti and half as a chilli con carne with half the amount of chilli powder and half a can of beans (use the rest of the beans to make a salad with one of the dressings on p56).

INDIAN SHEPHERD'S PIE Serves 4

I doubt if any self-respecting Indian shepherd would recognise this but it's good nonetheless.

For the mash
About 750g old potatoes
1/4 tsp ground turmeric (optional)
2-3 tbsp low-fat yoghurt

Simple Spaghetti Bolognese
  sauce (*see* p92) with half the
  tomato and no oregano
2-3 tsp of balti masala mix or
  other good medium hot curry
  powder
75g frozen peas (optional)
1 clove of garlic, crushed
Salt and pepper
3 heaped tbsp finely chopped
  coriander

Peel the potatoes, cut into quarters or halves then put in a large saucepan with cold water to cover. Bring to the boil, add a little salt then cook for about 15-20 minutes until you can stick a knife into the pieces without any resistance. Meanwhile cook the bolognese sauce, using half the tomato and leaving out the oregano. Add the balti powder and peas, if using, when you add the garlic. Let the sauce cook until most of the tomato juice has been absorbed (about 15-20 minutes) then take off the heat and stir in the coriander. Tip the mince into a lightly oiled shallow ovenproof dish and turn the oven on to 200C/400F/Gas 6. Drain the potatoes in a colander or sieve, return to the pan and mash with a fork until smooth. Sprinkle over the turmeric if using, add the yoghurt and garlic, season with salt and pepper and mash again.

Spoon the mash in dollops over the top of the mince then spread it out with a fork until it covers the mince completely (you can make artistic patterns with the prongs). Bake the pie for 20-25 minutes until the top begins to brown. Leave it for 5 minutes (if you can) before serving with a salad.

• You can make a quick version of this by combining fried mince with a tin or half a large jar of medium hot curry sauce plus the fresh coriander and using a large pack of instant mash (*see* p110 – be sure to use the kind with flakes, not powder).

FRENCH SHEPHERD'S PIE

The French have a splendid version of shepherd's pie called Hachis Parmentier *which has the virtue of a double layer of mash.*

Make it the same way as the Indian Shepherd's Pie, leaving out the spice and replacing the coriander with a generous handful of chopped parsley (about half a large pack or bunch). Make double the amount of mash, beating in lots of butter (about 40g) and half a cup (about 125ml) warm milk (*see* **MASH** p110) instead of the turmeric and yoghurt. Line a well-buttered dish with half the mash, spoon over the mince filling then top with the remaining mash.

• *See also* Lasagne, p109.

Who doesn't love sausages?
You could eat them almost every day without getting bored there are so many different flavours now. But they often don't taste as good as they should because they're fried to a frazzle.

How to cook a sausage?
More slowly than you think is the answer. If you fry them fast they'll split. You don't need to prick them either (a relic from the post-World-War-Two years when they were full of fat). Simply fry them over a low to medium heat, turning them occasionally to brown them evenly. Could take a good 15-20 minutes, depending how thick they are – less, obviously, for thin chipolatas (see p166, The Ultimate Fry-Up).

CUMBERLAND SAUSAGES WITH RICH GUINNESS GRAVY
Serves 4-6

This is the best sausage recipe I've ever come up with. Don't be put off by the idea of Guinness – it actually makes the most fantastic dark, rich, sticky onion gravy that doesn't taste remotely of beer.

2 tbsp olive oil
A good slice (about 25g) butter
2 large Spanish onions (about 425-450g), peeled and finely sliced
2 tsp sugar
2 tsp plain flour
250ml original Guinness
225ml stock made with 1 tsp of Marmite or 1/2 beef stock cube
2 x 350-400g packs of Cumberland sausages or other traditional British sausages
Salt and pepper
2-3 tsp white or red wine vinegar or malt vinegar

Heat one tablespoon of the oil in a large frying pan, add the butter then when it has melted tip in the onions. Stir them so they're coated with the butter mixture, then cook slowly over a low heat for about 25-30 minutes until completely soft and quite brown. Sprinkle in the sugar, mix in well then turn the heat up and stir continuously for about 5 minutes until the onions are really brown and caramelised. Meanwhile bring the stock to the boil. Stir the flour into the onions and cook for a minute then add the stock and the Guinness. Bubble up for a minute or two then turn right down and leave to simmer. Meanwhile grill or fry the sausages using the remaining oil until browned on all sides. Check the seasoning of the onion gravy adding a little salt if needed and 2-3 teaspoons of white wine vinegar. Transfer the sausages to the gravy, spooning it over them thoroughly then continue to cook on a low heat for about 15-20 minutes until the sausages are cooked. Serve with mashed potatoes or colcannon (see p110).

CHORIZO AND BUTTER BEAN STEW Serves 4

Chorizo – a dried Spanish salami-style sausage flavoured with paprika – is a really useful ingredient to have in the fridge to rustle up a quick supper with a couple of cans of beans. Although it's quite expensive you don't need a lot.

100g chunk of chorizo or a
  100g pack of sliced chorizo
1 green or red pepper
1 tbsp olive oil
1 medium onion, peeled
  and roughly chopped
1-2 cloves of garlic
1 tsp sweet pimenton
  or 1/2 tsp paprika
1/2 a 400g can tomatoes
  or 1/2 a 500ml carton passata
  or creamed tomatoes
2 x 400g cans butter beans
  or chickpeas
1/3 large bunch or 20g pack of
  parsley or 5-6 green cabbage
  leaves, finely shredded

Remove the skin from the chorizo, slice, cut into strips, then into small dice. Cut the pepper into quarters, remove the white pith and seeds and chop roughly. Heat a wok or large saucepan, add the oil then add the chorizo, onion and pepper. Fry, stirring occasionally for 7-8 minutes until the onion and pepper start to brown. Add the garlic, pimenton and paprika and cook for a minute then tip in the chopped tomatoes and butter beans. Stir well and cook for another 10 minutes adding 3-4 tbsp of water if the sauce gets a bit dry. If you're using greens stir them in 5 minutes before you serve up or add the parsley just before serving. This goes well with a green salad.

SICILIAN SAUSAGE
PASTA Serves 4

This is a very strong, punchy pasta made with spicy sausages (I used Sicilian style ones, hence the name, but you could use any spicy sausage with a bit of chilli in it).
Too expensive to make from scratch if you don't already have some of the ingredients, but a recipe you'll love if you're an olive addict.

1 400g pack fresh
 spicy sausages
1 tbsp olive oil
2 level tbsp tomato paste
A small glass (125ml) dry
 white wine
1/2 400g tin chopped tomatoes
2 tbsp capers, well rinsed
 (optional)
10-12 green or black olives,
 pitted and roughly chopped
300g short, chunky pasta like
 rigatoni or penne
A good handful of parsley, finely
 chopped (about 4tbsp)
A pinch of chilli powder or a few
 drops of hot pepper sauce
100g white crumbly cheese
 like Caerphilly, Cheshire or
 Wensleydale
Salt and pepper

Using a small sharp knife, cut a slit in the sausage skins and peel them off. Heat the oil in a large frying pan and add the sausages, breaking them up as you go with a wooden spoon. Add the tomato paste, stir in well and fry for a minute or two. Add the white wine, let it sizzle and die down then add the tinned tomatoes. Break them down with a fork, together with any larger pieces of sausage meat. Add the capers and olives, stir then leave to simmer for about 15 minutes. Meanwhile boil the pasta in salted water until just cooked, spooning off 2-3 spoonfuls of the cooking water into the pasta sauce. Drain the pasta and tip it into the pasta sauce. Add half the parsley, mix in well and leave to stand for a couple of minutes for the flavours to amalgamate. Check seasoning adding salt, pepper and extra chilli powder if needed. Break the cheese up roughly with a fork. Divide the pasta between 4 plates, crumble over some cheese and sprinkle over the remaining parsley.

WARM POTATO AND SAUSAGE SALAD

Serves 2-4

If you think salad is for rabbits this one's for you. It's the kind of meal to eat on a Saturday afternoon in front of the telly with a can (or two) of lager.

About 400g new potatoes or, at a pinch, 2 small cans of new potatoes
Salt and freshly ground black pepper
A double quantity of the French-Style Mustard Dressing (*see* p56)
150g chunk of garlic sausage or bierwurst, skin removed and cut into small chunks or a pack of sliced garlic sausage, cut into strips
1 small onion or half a medium onion, peeled and finely chopped
About 8-10 small cornichons or gherkins, finely sliced or 2 large pickled cucumbers finely chopped
2-3 tbsp finely chopped parsley

Scrub or wash the new potatoes if necessary and cut into even-sized pieces. Boil a large kettle of water, pour into a saucepan, bring back to the boil, add a little salt and tip in the new potatoes. Cook for about 10 minutes till you can stick a knife in them without any resistance. (Or heat the tinned potatoes following the instructions on the can.) Drain and cool for 5 or 10 minutes then chop the potatoes roughly and toss with the mustard dressing. Mix with the garlic sausage, onion and either the cornichons or gherkins. Check the seasoning, adding salt and pepper to taste and a splash of liquid from the pickled cucumber or cornichon jar if you think it needs zipping up. Sprinkle over parsley and serve.

• You could also make this salad with frankfurters, cooked vegetarian sausages or, come to think of it, Spam.

There's no point in making a stew if you're in a hurry. Or if you can't be bothered faffing around with the preparation it involves. True you can buy ready-prepared stewing steak and packs of stewing veg but they'll cost twice as much (though don't let me stop you if that doesn't worry you). The beauty about stews is that the long slow cooking (the surface of the stew should barely tremble) makes even cheap cuts of meat tender, so it really is a bargain meal. And a delicious one.

A GOOD OLD-FASHIONED PUB STEW Serves 4-6

Leg of beef is one of the best cuts to use for stew. Don't worry about the tough looking lines of what looks like gristle in the meat. It all melts down in the cooking giving you a fantastically rich gravy. But do trim off the excess fat.

1 kg stewing beef
  (e.g. leg of beef)
2 tbsp plain flour
4-5 tbsp sunflower or olive oil
3-4 medium onions
  (about 400-450g)
4 medium to large carrots
  (400-450g)
A couple of sprigs of fresh
  thyme or 1/2 tsp dried thyme
  or herbes de Provence
  (optional)
250ml stock made with 1 tsp
  Marmite dissolved in 250ml
  boiling water
250ml ale or dry cider
Salt and pepper and maybe
  a little extra Marmite, wine
  vinegar and/or a few drops
  of Worcestershire Sauce

Cut the beef up into large chunks removing the more obvious bits of fat. (If you only have a blunt knife this may be easier with kitchen scissors). Put the flour in a shallow dish and season with salt and pepper. Toss half the meat in the flour until it is thoroughly coated. Heat a large frying pan on the hob, add 2 tablespoons of oil and fry the floured meat on all sides until browned (about 5 minutes). Spoon the meat into a large saucepan or casserole dish. Toss the remaining meat in flour, add another spoonful of oil to the frying pan, fry the rest of the meat and transfer to the casserole or pan. Meanwhile peel the onions and slice them thickly. Add 2 more tablespoons of oil to the frying pan and fry the onions gently for about 10 minutes until soft. Peel and slice the carrots and add them to the pan for the last 5 minutes along with the thyme and any flour left over from coating the meat. Pour in the hot stock and beer or cider and bring to the boil then pour over the meat.

Bring the stew back to the boil then turn the heat right down so that it bubbles very, very gently. Cover the pan and leave it to cook, stirring occasionally for about 2½ hours. If the sauce seems too thin take off the cover for about 1 hour before the end of cooking time. Check the meat is cooked (it should be soft enough to cut with a fork) and adjust the seasoning. It'll probably need 1-1½ teaspoons more of Marmite (dissolved in a tablespoon of hot water) and ½ teaspoon of Worcestershire Sauce if you've got some. And maybe a teaspoon of vinegar to sharpen it up. Serve with baked or boiled potatoes.

• If you can leave it overnight before you eat it'll taste even better.

UNE DAUBE 'SUPER'

To make a stew or daube the French way substitute half a bottle of full-bodied red wine and a small wineglass of water (about 125ml) for the beer and stock. Add two crushed cloves of garlic when you add the herbs plus a handful of black olives if you're into olives. Correct the seasoning at the end of the cooking time with about a tablespoon of tomato ketchup or tomato paste rather than Marmite or Worcestershire Sauce and stir in 3 tablespoons chopped parsley. This goes better with mash or tagliatelle.

There are probably more special offers on chicken than any other food – the problem is most of it is intensively reared. In general I think it's better to buy a large pack of free-range chicken thighs and drumsticks than a bog-standard chicken breast (though breast is undoubtedly best if you want a small amount for a soup, stir-fry or salad).

SWEET CHICKEN WITH MIRACLE PEPPER SAUCE

Serves 4 (or up to 8 at a stretch; see Triple Carbo Trick, below)

My husband tells me great tales of the girls he impressed with this recipe when he was at university (the miracle not in the fact that he pulled but that this sauce virtually makes itself). Though there's a bit of preliminary preparation involved, once it's cooking you can just leave it.

2 tbsp flour
1 kg chicken thighs and drumsticks, preferably free-range
5 tbsp oil
3-4 medium onions (about 400g), peeled, halved and sliced
3 medium to large mixed peppers (red, yellow and green or just red and yellow)
1 small can or ½ 400g can of chopped tomatoes
1 tsp fresh thyme or ½ tsp dried thyme or oregano
½ tsp hot paprika or 1 tsp mild paprika
Salt and pepper

Put the flour in a shallow bowl and season with salt and pepper. Dip the chicken pieces in the flour and coat thoroughly. Shake off the excess flour. Heat 2 tablespoons of oil in a wok or large frying pan and fry 4 of the pieces on both sides until well browned (about 2 minutes a side). Remove them from the pan, set aside on a plate and repeat with the other chicken pieces. Take them out of the pan and put them on the plate too. Pour away the fat in the pan (it'll be pretty mucky by now) rinse the pan and dry with kitchen towel. Pour the remainder of the oil in the pan, add the onions and stir to coat with oil. Leave them cooking while you quarter the peppers, remove the white pithy bits and cut into thick slices. Add them to the onions, mix in and continue to cook for a couple of minutes.

Put the chicken back in the pan mixing it in with the onions and peppers then turn the heat down, put a lid on or large piece of foil over the wok and leave to cook for about 20 minutes, turning the chicken pieces over a couple of times. After a while you'll find that the onions and peppers have miraculously produced a sauce. Add the tomatoes, thyme and paprika, mix in well then replace the lid and continue to cook on a low heat for another 40 minutes or until the chicken is beginning to fall away from the bones. Check the seasoning, adding salt and pepper to taste. Serve with pasta, rice, or boiled/new potatoes – or all three.

The Triple Carbo Trick

- If you want to make this dish (or similar main courses) go further the trick is to make a lot of sauce then lay on lavish amounts of carbohydrate. I had a similar dish in a French brasserie once with pasta, chips *and* beans.

Cook-in sauces

- There's no point in pretending there aren't times when we all fall back on a cook-in sauce, especially with chicken. But some are a lot better than others and even the best (Loyd Grossman, Pataks) need tweaking slightly if they're to taste home-made. Tomato-based sauces usually benefit from a bit of extra garlic, some chopped parsley and a few drops of lemon juice or vinegar. You can liven up curry sauces with lemon juice, yoghurt and coriander. Look out for special offers on sauces. At the full price they're expensive.

BAKED CHICKEN WITH GARLIC AND LOVELY LEMONY POTATOES

Serves 4

Good enough to be a feast. Irresistible enough to want to make most weeks. Do use free-range chicken if you can possibly afford it.

4 medium to large potatoes (about 600-700g)
2-3 tbsp olive oil plus a little soft butter
Salt and pepper
1 large lemon, preferably unwaxed
2-3 cloves of garlic
2-3 sprigs of fresh rosemary or thyme or 1 tsp dried oregano
4 chicken quarters (about 1 kg in total) or 1 kg chicken thighs and drumsticks

Heat the oven to 200°C/400°F/Gas 6. Peel and cut the potatoes into thick slices (slightly thicker than a pound coin). Generously smear a roasting tin with soft butter or olive oil and lay the potato slices in a single layer over the base. Season with salt and pepper. Cut half the lemon into thin slices, halve them and lay the pieces over the potatoes. Peel and finely slice the garlic and strip the leaves from the rosemary and scatter them both over the top. Pour over a couple of tablespoons of water. Cut any loose bits of skin off the chicken pieces and lay them skin side down over the potatoes. Squeeze the juice from the remaining half of the lemon over the chicken, drizzle over a tablespoon of olive oil and season with salt and pepper. Bake in the oven for half an hour then turn the chicken pieces over, spoon the pan juices over them and season again with salt and pepper. Turn the oven down to 190°C/375°F/Gas 5 and continue to cook for about

25-30 minutes until the chicken is well browned and the potato cooked through. (Spoon off a couple of tablespoons of the cooking juices about 10 minutes before the chicken is ready, to crisp the potatoes up.) Fish out the lemon slices when you serve up. This tastes good with any green vegetable, especially broccoli, spinach and beans or with a salad.

(*See also* No-Carve Roast Chicken Dinner, p128.)

CHICKEN SATAY
SALAD Serves 4-6

This is one of those infinitely flexible recipes that you can make depending on what you have to hand or can afford. Make it with cold or leftover chicken, with any kind of crunchy salad or veg.
Varying the dressing to taste (though the peanut butter is non-negotiable). Here's how to make it from scratch.

2 skinless, boneless chicken breasts or 4 chicken thighs or a 375g-400g pack of stir-fry chicken or turkey
2 tbsp sunflower or olive oil
3 tbsp light soy sauce
1 dessertspoon of runny honey or 2 tsp sugar
1/3-1/2 a jar (about 110g) smooth or crunchy peanut butter (I like Whole Earth)
2 tbsp sweet chilli sauce
1 tbsp lime or lemon juice
2 cloves of garlic, peeled and crushed
Salt and pepper
1/2 a large cucumber
2 medium-sized carrots
1/2 pack (about 125g) beansprouts or 2-3 sticks of celery and/or a green or red pepper
Half a bunch of spring onions (optional)
About 3 tbsp chopped coriander leaves (optional)

Cut the chicken into thin strips. Heat a large frying pan or wok, add the oil, tip in the chicken and stir-fry for about 2 minutes. Add the soy sauce, a tablespoon of water and the honey and continue to fry until the liquid evaporates and the chicken starts to get brown and sticky. Spoon the chicken onto a plate, chuck a small glass (about 125ml) of water into the pan, stir to loosen any tasty sticky bits and set on one side. Scoop the peanut butter into a bowl and add the pan juices to make a thick sauce. Add the sweet chilli sauce, the remaining garlic and soy sauce and about 1 tablespoon of lime or lemon juice. Taste and adjust the seasoning adding salt and pepper to taste. Cut the cucumber into four lengthways, cut away the seeds and cut into fine strips about the size of a match. Peel and slice the carrots and celery, if using, into thin strips too. Wash the beansprouts. Trim the roots and half the green tops off the spring onions, quarter them lengthways and cut into four. Mix all the veg in a large bowl with the chicken and pour over enough dressing to coat the salad without drowning it. (Any leftover dressing can be used as a dip with raw vegetables.) Scatter over the coriander if using.

! Do not give this salad to anyone who is allergic to peanuts.

Two of the most comforting meals of all – macaroni cheese and cauliflower cheese – involve knowing how to make a classic cheese sauce. Which is not that difficult – you just need to do it once or twice to feel confident about it.

CLASSIC CHEESE SAUCE 🍁 Serves 4

This requires your undivided attention for 5 minutes. Don't get distracted or lumps will ensue.

40g butter
3 tbsp (40g) plain flour
1 small 584 ml carton of
  semi-skimmed or ordinary milk
  (but not skimmed)
75g strong or 100g medium
  Cheddar, coarsely grated
Salt and pepper

Cut the butter into chunks and melt gently in a medium-sized non-stick saucepan. Take the pan off the heat and stir the flour into the butter with a wooden spoon until it is smooth. Put the pan back on a low heat for a few seconds to 'cook' the flour and butter mixture, stirring it all the time, then remove it from the heat again. Add the milk bit by bit stirring to amalgamate it completely before you add the next lot. (Don't worry if it suddenly goes very thick. Keep stirring and gradually adding the milk). Leave about 100ml of the milk in the carton for the moment. Put the pan back on the hob, increase the heat slightly then bring the milk gradually to the boil stirring all the time. You should end up with a satiny smooth sauce. Turn the heat right down again and leave the sauce to simmer for 5 minutes, stirring it occasionally. Add the grated cheese and stir till smooth again. Stir in a little extra milk if the sauce seems too thick (it should just coat the back of your spoon without running off it) and let it cook for a moment. Season to taste with salt and pepper.

! Use a non-stick saucepan. It'll stop the sauce sticking to the base of the pan and leaving brown bits through your sauce.

! If the sauce goes lumpy all is not lost. Force it through a fine sieve. You'll get slightly less sauce but it will at least be edible.

CLASSIC MACARONI

CHEESE   Serves 4

Although I ca**V** his macaroni cheese it's actually better made with a thicker pasta like penne or rigatoni.

3 tbsp butter (40g) plus a bit
   for buttering the baking dish
3 tbsp (40g) plain flour
A small (584ml) carton of milk
150g strong Cheddar, coarsely
   grated
Salt and freshly ground black
   pepper
350g penne or rigatoni
1 tsp Dijon mustard or ½ tsp
   English mustard (optional)

Make the base for the sauce as described opposite then leave it over a low heat without adding the cheese while you cook the pasta. Bring a large pan of water to the boil, add salt then tip in the pasta, stir and cook for the time recommended on the pack. Just before the pasta is ready, stir half the cheese into the sauce together with the mustard, if using, and season with salt and pepper. Drain the pasta thoroughly and pour into a lightly buttered shallow baking dish. Pour over the cheese sauce and mix it in well. Sprinkle over the remains of the grated cheese. Place the dish under a hot grill for about 5 minutes until the top is brown and crispy. If you don't have a grill, bake in a hot oven (200°C/400°F/Gas 6) for about 15-20 minutes until browned.

- I'm a bit of a purist about macaroni cheese but you can of course add other things to it – ham, crisp fried bacon bits, mushrooms, a layer of sliced tomatoes over the top, whatever. The best alternative version is to cook a couple of washed, sliced leeks (*see* p31) in the butter before you add the flour then add the milk as usual (you may need slightly more).
- You can substitute other hard cheeses, but make sure they're medium or strong in flavour. Lancashire is good or Red Leicester.
- Use this recipe if you want to make cauliflower cheese (*see* p31 for how to prepare and cook a cauliflower).

LIGHT LEEKS WITH CREAMY DOLCELATTE SAUCE ☘ Serves 2

The healthiness of the leeks makes up for the indulgence of the creamy Dolcelatte. Because it's rather a luxurious dish I'm suggesting it for two instead of four.

4 medium-sized leeks or 3 big ones (about 450-500g)
150g Dolcelatte or mild Gorgonzola cheese
1 small (142ml) carton of whipping cream or double cream
A little lemon juice to taste (optional)
Freshly ground black pepper
2 tbsp freshly grated Parmesan or 3tbsp grated Caerphilly or Wensleydale

Cut the roots off the leeks then trim off about half the green leaves at the top. Cut them in half lengthways and hold them under running water to clean them thoroughly washing off any grit between the leaves. Cut the larger leeks lengthways in half again then cut each piece into three. Lay the leeks in a small microwaveable dish and add 3 tablespoons of water. Cover with cling film, pierce, then microwave at full power for 3 minutes. Check to see how they're getting on and give them another minute or two if necessary. You want them to be just tender. Drain them in a colander or sieve then return to the dish. Meanwhile cut any rind off the Dolcelatte and mash with 2 tablespoons of the cream. Tip into a small saucepan and heat gently stirring occasionally till the cheese has melted. Add another 3-4 tablespoons of cream until it looks like a sauce. Check seasoning adding black pepper and – if you think it needs it – a little lemon juice to taste. Pour the sauce over the leeks, top with the grated cheese and place the dish under the grill until the top is brown and bubbling. This would go well with some crusty bread or brown rice. It also works really well as a filling for baked potatoes in which case it would serve four.

- You could also use this sauce for cauliflower or broccoli.
- Add some chopped ham for a non-veggie version.
- If you don't have a microwave you could steam the leeks instead, or just cook them in a little water in a covered pan over a very gentle heat.

PROPER HOME-MADE LASAGNE Serves 4 or – less likely I admit – possibly 6

I wasn't going to put this in because you can buy perfectly good lasagne in the shops and it is hard work and time-consuming to make. But there were vociferous protests at home so I relented. It is worth soaking the lasagne even if the pack says it's ready to cook otherwise it always seems to go hard and cardboardy.

Simple Spaghetti Bolognese
    sauce (*see* p92), except use
    half the amount of tomatoes
Classic Cheese Sauce
    (*see* p106) using half the cheese
    – and don't add it yet (*see* right)
½ 500g-pack of dried lasagne
    (about 9 sheets)
A little soft butter and a little
    extra milk

First make the bolognese sauce and leave it to cook over a low heat. Then make the base for the cheese sauce but don't add any cheese yet. Fill a large pan full of boiling water (from the kettle) and drop the lasagne sheets in one by one. Let them soak until soft (about 2-3 minutes) then drain them in a colander or sieve and rinse them under a cold tap, making sure they don't stick together. Heat the oven to 200°C/400°F/ Gas 6. Smear soft butter round the sides of a medium-sized square or rectangular ovenproof dish. (A roasting tin is a bit too big.) Tip two thirds of the cheese sauce base into the bolognese sauce and mix well. Add about 25g of grated cheese to the remaining sauce and keep warm. Take a spoonful of bolognese sauce and spread it over the base of the baking dish. Arrange a third of the lasagne sheets in a single layer on top, trimming them with a knife or scissors to make them fit.

Top with half the remaining bolognese plus another layer of lasagne then repeat with the remaining bolognese and lasagne sheets. Stir a little extra milk into the cheese sauce (about 2-3 tablespoons) to thin it out then pour it over the top of the lasagne, spreading it evenly so all the pasta is covered. Sprinkle with the remaining grated cheese and bake for about 30-40 minutes until the top is well browned.

• You could use Quorn or soy
  mince instead of beef.

PERFECT MASHED POTATO Serves 4

Even though you can use packet mash and now chilled and frozen mash, nothing is as good (or as cheap) as the real thing.

1 kg King Edward or other good boiling potatoes (now marked on supermarket packs)
A good slice (25g) of butter
50-75ml warm milk
Salt and freshly ground black pepper

Peel the potatoes and halve or quarter them so you have even sized pieces. Put them in a saucepan of cold water and bring them to the boil (about 5 minutes). Skim off any froth, season them with salt then cook them for 20-25 minutes until you can put the tip of a knife into them without any resistance. Drain the potatoes thoroughly in a colander then return them to the pan and put it back over the heat for a few seconds to dry up any excess moisture.

Take the pan off the heat, chop the potatoes up roughly with a knife, then mash them with a potato masher or a fork until they are smooth and lump free. Beat in the remaining butter and enough milk to make a soft but not sloppy consistency (unless, like the French, you like your mash sloppy). Season with salt and freshly ground black pepper plus any of the suggested seasonings (right).

! Don't be tempted to put potatoes in a food processor or liquidiser. They'll go horribly gluey.

! New potatoes don't mash well. Instead boil them and crush them in a hot pan with a little olive oil, butter and fresh parsley and a squeeze of lemon.

What you can add to mash
- A teaspoon or two of Dijon mustard, creamed horseradish or pesto.
- A tablespoon of Parmesan or 2 tablespoons of other hard grated cheese.
- A couple of tablespoonfuls of double cream or crème fraîche instead of some of the milk.
- Add a couple of cloves of garlic to the water when you cook the potatoes then mash them with the potatoes for garlic mash.
- Some lightly cooked chopped greens or shredded cabbage, tossed in a little butter (called colcannon in Ireland).
- 1-2 leeks, cleaned (*see* p31), chopped and cooked in a little butter.

How to tart up packet mash

It may lack the irresistibly fluffy texture of the real thing but packet mash can be made to taste almost as good. Choose the French kind which is made from flakes rather than Smash-type granules and make it slightly sloppier than you would home-made mash. Be generous with the butter and other seasonings.

Root veg mash

Root veg like carrots, parsnips, celeriac and swede also make good mash, though carrots and celeriac are best combined with another mashed vegetable like swedes (good with carrots) or potato (with celeriac). Swedes however, which are known as neeps north of the border, are a triumph on their own (and the classic accompaniment to haggis).

BASHED NEEPS WITH CRISPY BACON Serves 4

2 medium or 1 large swede
1 litre of light vegetable stock made with 1 tbsp vegetable bouillon powder or a vegetable stock cube
Salt, freshly ground black pepper
A pinch of ground nutmeg (optional)
A good slice of butter (about 40g)
2 tbsp cooking oil
A 225g pack of streaky bacon

Cut the swedes into quarters and peel them (you'll need a sharp knife as their skin is quite tough). Cut them into large cubes, put them in a saucepan, add enough stock or water to cover them (about a litre) and boil till they are tender. Drain them, reserving the cooking liquid and either whizz them in a food processor or with a handheld blender, or mash (bash) them by hand with a potato masher or a fork. Add a bit of the cooking liquid and the butter to get a smooth texture then season them well with salt, freshly ground black pepper and, ideally, a little ground nutmeg. Taste, adjust the seasoning if necessary and keep warm while you heat the oil and fry the bacon until crisp (see p166 for tips). This also goes well with buttered cabbage (see p30).

• Nutmeg also goes very well with spinach and in cheese sauces. It's quite expensive but you need very little.

I'm referring to potatoes, of course....

Hashes are a great way of using up leftover potato but are still worth making even if you have to cook them from scratch.

CHILLI BEEF HASH
Serves 4

This is a zipped-up version of that great American store cupboard standby – corned beef hash. If you haven't got any cooked potatoes boil some first.

2 tbsp oil
1 large onion, peeled and roughly chopped or a bunch of spring onions, trimmed and sliced into thin rings
2 cloves of garlic, peeled and crushed
1 tsp smoked pimenton (Spanish paprika), paprika or mild chilli powder
1 tin of corned beef, cut into large cubes
3 medium to large cooked potatoes (about 600g), roughly chopped
3 heaped tbsp chopped fresh parsley
Salt

Heat the oil in a large frying pan or wok. Cook the onion over a moderate heat until beginning to brown (about 6-7 minutes). Add the garlic and 1-2 teaspoons of pimenton or paprika (depending how hot it is) and cook for another minute then add the corned beef and potatoes. Break them up roughly with a spatula then turn the heat up and cook, turning the mixture over occasionally until it begins to form a crust (about 5-8 minutes). Add the chopped parsley and season with salt and a little extra pimenton if you think it needs it. Serve on its own with ketchup or with a fried egg on top.

- To make it healthier, replace the parsley with 1/2 pack of lightly cooked chopped greens or 1/2 small green cabbage, finely sliced and cooked in boiling water for 2 minutes.
- To make it stretch add a can of drained red kidney beans or borlotti beans at the same time you add the beef and potato.

You can also make a good hash with...
- Equal quantities of leftover potatoes and cabbage cooked in oil butter and seasoned with salt and plenty of pepper (bubble and squeak).
- Bacon, cooked potatoes and onions (*see also* Frittatas, p55).
- Chopped chorizo, cooked potatoes, onions, garlic and green pepper.

SALMON AND LEEK HASH Serves 3-4

This is a ritzier, less rustic kind of hash – a bit like a deconstructed fishcake. You could also make it with tinned salmon, which would be cheaper and taste just as good. But I must confess I have a problem with the smell of canned salmon.

450-500g uncooked – or cooked – new potatoes
250g-300g cooked or uncooked boneless, skinless salmon fillet or a pack of smoked trout
2 medium leeks, cleaned and chopped (*see* p31)
1 tbsp olive oil
A slice of butter (about 25g)
1/2 small packet of fresh dill or 3 tbsp chopped fresh parsley
About 1 tbsp lemon juice
Salt and freshly ground black pepper
A small carton of sour cream (optional)

Boil the potatoes in salted boiling water until just tender (about 12-15 minutes). Drain and set aside until cool enough to handle. Meanwhile microwave or steam the salmon and break it into chunks with a fork. Clean and slice the leeks (*see* p31). Heat a large frying pan or wok over a moderate heat then add the oil and the butter. Gently cook the sliced leeks for about 5 minutes until they are beginning to soften but still green. Slice the potatoes thickly and add to the pan. Crush them roughly with a fork and fry with the leeks for about 5 minutes until beginning to brown. Add the salmon and heat through, turning the mixture carefully with a fork so as not to break it up too much. Strip the dill leaves from the stalks and chop them or snip them finely with scissors. Sprinkle half the dill over the hash and season it with lemon juice, salt and black pepper. Divide the hash onto plates, spooning a little sour cream over the top of each serving and sprinkle with the remaining dill.

- Dill also goes brilliantly with a cucumber salad.

I'm sure we'd all eat more rice if it wasn't so confusing. Nowadays there are about 20 different types to choose from. The ones you're most likely to come across are:

Basmati rice
Well worth the extra money, especially to go with a curry (see Perfect fluffy rice, below), it has the best flavour and texture of any rice.

Easy-cook rice
Cheaper but doesn't have nearly such a good flavour. Works well for flavoured rice, though personally I'd use Basmati or ordinary long-grain rice.

Instant rice
Frozen rice is fine though expensive. 'Express' sachets are less appetising, though they are useful for late night fuel.

Thai jasmine rice
The authentic rice to accompany Thai dishes. Slightly sticky which always makes you feel that you haven't cooked it properly. Again, you can substitute Basmati.

Brown rice
Like brown flour or wholewheat pasta, brown rice contains the whole grain which gives it a distinctive nutty flavour. Good for salads but takes at least twice as long to cook as ordinary rice.

Short-grain or pudding rice
For traditional English rice puddings. Don't bother – buy a tin. And don't use it for savoury dishes or risottos.

Risotto rice
Also labelled Arborio, Carnaroli and Vialone Nano. Pricey but essential if you want to make an authentic risotto (*see* p160). (*See* barlotto recipes, pp118-119, for a cheaper alternative.)

PERFECT FLUFFY RICE

The best type of rice to go with a curry. The key to making it fluffy is to cook it in lots of water like pasta. Measure out about 60g of Basmati or other long grain rice per person, tip it into a saucepan of boiling, salted water, stir once then boil for 10 minutes. Drain in a colander or sieve then balance the sieve over the saucepan and cover it with a piece of kitchen towel. After 5 minutes, pour away any water that has accumulated in the pan, tip in the rice and fork it through to fluff it up.

FLAVOURED RICE

If you want your rice flavoured with spices, onions or other flavourings you need to measure the water you put in it exactly and cook it in a pan with a lid on until it has absorbed. The easiest way to do this is to measure both the rice and the liquid in a measuring jug (twice as much liquid as rice).

PRAWN AND PEA PILAU Serves 4

A light fresh Indian-style rice dish which you could eat on its own or as an accompaniment to a fish curry. I don't normally go for ready-made spice mixes but Schwartz's pilau rice seasoning is a good one.

4 tbsp sunflower or olive oil
1 medium onion, finely chopped
2 tsp pilau rice seasoning or mild curry powder
250ml Basmati rice (measured in a jug)
1 clove of garlic, peeled and crushed
200g fresh or defrosted frozen prawns
125g defrosted frozen peas
Salt and freshly squeezed lemon juice to taste

Heat 2 tablespoons of the oil in a saucepan. Cook the onion over a medium heat for about 7-8 minutes stirring occasionally until it starts to brown. Add a heaped teaspoon of the pilau rice seasoning, stir and cook for a minute. Then add the rice, stir, cook a further minute and pour in 500ml of boiling water. Stir once, cover the pan tightly with a lid or a piece of foil, turn the heat down and cook for about 15 minutes until the water has been absorbed. Meanwhile heat the remaining oil in a small frying pan. Add the remaining teaspoon of pilau rice seasoning, cook for a minute then add the crushed garlic and prawns. Stir-fry for a couple of minutes then add the peas and leave on a low heat. When the rice is cooked mix the prawn and pea mixture into the rice, replace the lid and leave off the heat for 5 minutes. Check the seasoning, adding a squeeze of lemon juice and salt to taste.

Leftover rice

- As useful as leftover pasta or potatoes. You can make a rice salad with it (add the dressing while the rice is still warm) or fry it up like a hash.

! If you don't have a microwave you can defrost the prawns and peas by simply pouring boiling water over them and leaving them a couple of minutes.

PRAWN AND EGG-FRIED RICE

Serves 2-3

Another spin on the prawn and pea combo – this time Chinese. Don't attempt to make it with rice you've just cooked or it'll go soggy.

4 spring onions or 1 small onion, peeled and finely chopped
75g frozen peas
75g fresh or frozen prawns, thawed
2 large or 3 medium eggs
1 tsp Thai fish sauce (optional)
Salt for seasoning
2 tbsp oil
About 275g cold, cooked Basmati rice (about 125g of uncooked rice)
1-1½ tbsp soy sauce

Trim the roots off the spring onions and the top half of the green leaves. Peel off any damaged leaves and slice into thin rounds. Microwave the peas with 2 tablespoons of water or cook them for 2 minutes in boiling water and drain. Defrost the prawns in a microwave or heat them gently in a saucepan until just thawed and drain. Beat the eggs lightly with the fish sauce or a little salt. Heat a wok over a moderate heat and pour in the oil.
Tip in the onions and stir-fry for 2-3 minutes until beginning to brown. Add the peas and eggs and stir until almost all the liquid egg has disappeared. Add the rice and prawns and stir-fry for a couple of minutes until hot through. Add soy sauce to taste and serve.

• If you haven't got any prawns you can make this with a couple of slices of chopped ham.

❀Veggies can obviously leave out the prawns.

PAELLA Serves 6

Well, not quite paella, but near enough. Don't feel you have to include every ingredient I've listed. Just adapt it depending on what you've got in the fridge.

2 tbsp oil
90-100g chunk of chorizo or Pepperoni sausage cut into small dice
1 onion, peeled and roughly chopped or 5-6 spring onions, trimmed and finely sliced
1 red pepper, deseeded and chopped and/or 3 sticks of celery, finely sliced
1 cooked chicken breast or 2 cooked chicken thighs cut into small chunks
2 cloves of garlic, peeled and crushed
$1/2$ tsp turmeric
$1/2$ tsp sweet pimenton or paprika (double this if using pepperoni)
250g Basmati rice or ordinary long-grain rice
$1/2$ 400g tin of chopped tomatoes
600ml hot stock made with 2 tsp vegetable bouillon or a chicken or vegetable stock cube
125g frozen prawns, defrosted
100g frozen peas, defrosted
Salt and freshly ground black pepper
1-1$1/2$ tbsp lemon juice
4 heaped tbsp chopped fresh parsley (optional)

Heat a wok and add the oil. Chuck in the chorizo and stir for a minute, then add the onion and a minute later the peppers. Stir-fry for about 4-5 minutes until they start to soften and brown. Add the chicken, garlic and spices, stir and cook for a minute then add the rice, stir, then the tomatoes and stock. Turn the heat down and cook the paella gently for about 20 minutes, giving an occasional stir to stop the rice sticking to the base of the pan (but don't stir it like a risotto). When the liquid is nearly absorbed add the prawns and peas and cook for a further 4-5 minutes until there is no liquid left. Season with salt, pepper and lemon juice, stir in the parsley then cover the pan and leave it for 5-10 minutes for the flavours to absorb and the rice to fluff up.

• If you want to make this from uncooked chicken, cut a breast or two thighs into strips and stir-fry it before you add the chorizo.

Somebody, some day is going to decide that pearl barley is a cool ingredient. In the meantime take advantage of the fact that it's the cheapest carbohydrate around.

MUSHROOM BARLOTTO 🍁🍁 Serves 4

Weird name you might think but this is basically a cross between a risotto and a pilaf only made with pearl barley which is a fraction of the price of Arborio rice. I could have called it barlaf I suppose but barlotto sounded better. This whole meal won't cost much more than 30p a head and will feed four hungry people. And it's OK for vegans and the wheat- and dairy-intolerant. How virtuous can you get?

2 tbsp sunflower oil or olive oil
2 medium or 1 large onion, peeled and chopped as small as you can
About 150g mushrooms, rinsed clean and roughly chopped
3 sticks of celery, trimmed and finely sliced
2 cloves of garlic, crushed
1/4 tsp hot paprika or cayenne pepper
1 tsp each of ground cumin and coriander
250g pearl barley
1/2 400g tin chopped tomatoes
Salt
1/2 large bunch or a small packet of fresh coriander or coriander and parsley leaves, roughly chopped.

Heat the oil over a moderate heat in a large saucepan. Add the chopped onion, stir and cook gently for about 5 minutes until soft. Add the chopped mushrooms, celery and garlic and continue to cook for another 5 minutes, stirring occasionally. Add the spices, pearl barley and chopped tomatoes and stir, then pour in 500ml of boiling water. Bring back to the boil then cover, turn the heat right down and simmer for about 25-30 minutes, stirring occasionally until almost all the water is absorbed. Check seasoning, adding salt to taste then chuck in the chopped herbs. Stir and serve.

LEEK AND BACON BARLOTTO Serves 4

Creamier and more like a conventional risotto. Obviously leave out the bacon for a vegetarian version.

2 large leeks (preferably with
  some green leaves)
2 tbsp olive or sunflower oil
4-5 streaky bacon rashers, rinded
  and cut into small pieces or
  about 125g bacon bits
  (if you use offcuts make sure
  you trim most of the fat off)
250g pearl barley
500ml stock made with 2 tsp
  of vegetable bouillon powder
3-4 tbsp freshly grated
  Parmesan or grano padano
  plus extra for serving
1 heaped tbsp crème fraîche
  or Quark
Salt and freshly ground pepper

Cut the roots and about half of the green tops of the leeks off and strip off the outer layer. Slice the leeks into rounds then wash under running water or in a large bowl of cold water, making sure you remove all the grit. Heat the oil in a large saucepan then add the bacon and fry until it begins to brown. Add the leeks, stir, cover the pan with a lid or a piece of foil and cook for 5 minutes until they begin to soften. Stir in the barley then pour in the stock. Bring to the boil, reduce the heat to low and leave to cook, stirring occasionally until the barley is soft and the liquid has been absorbed. Stir in the Parmesan and some crème fraîche if you have some. Season with pepper and serve in bowls with extra grated cheese.

- Quark is a light, tangy low-fat cheese which tastes a bit like Philadelphia cream cheese. It's also very good on crispbreads and crackers.

Instant couscous – the most common type you'll find in supermarkets – is as quick and easy as instant mash but a lot nicer. Get into the habit of using it as an alternative to rice or the base of a salad. Don't bother with the flavoured ones which are – inevitably – more expensive. It's easy enough to doctor your own with a little olive oil and fresh herbs.

MOROCCAN SPICED FISH WITH CORIANDER AND COUSCOUS Serves 4

Don't hesitate to use basic frozen fish steaks for this. Even though they look like a brick they'll taste good.

250g instant couscous
5 tbsp olive oil
Juice of one lemon (about 3 tbsp)
2 cloves of garlic
1½ tsp Moroccan spice mix (*see* p35)
Salt and pepper
4 tbsp finely chopped fresh coriander or parsley or a mixture of the two
4 chunky cod, haddock or hoki fillets (about 600g) or 4 defrosted frozen fish steaks

Pour 3 tablespoons of the olive oil, the lemon juice, crushed garlic, spices, salt and 2 tablespoons of the chopped coriander into a shallow ovenproof dish. Whisk together, then add the cod steaks and turn them in the marinade so they're thoroughly coated.

If you have time leave them covered in the fridge for an hour or so for the flavours to infuse. Heat the oven to 200°C/400°F/Gas 6. Turn the fillets skin sides upwards, put the dish in the oven and roast for 10 minutes. Turn the fish carefully with a fish slice and spoon over the marinade then roast for a further 8-12 minutes depending on the thickness of the fillets. (They should have turned white but still be quite firm.) Meanwhile prepare the couscous according to the instructions on the packet. When it has absorbed the water, fork it through to fluff it up and drizzle over a couple of tablespoons of olive oil. Add the remaining herbs, fork it through again then warm it gently over a low heat. Serve with the fish and a salad.

- You could also bake cod or other white fish in the Easiest Ever Pasta Sauce (*see* p44) adding a few olives and capers.

CUCUMBER, HERB AND COUSCOUS SALAD V Ve Serves 4-6

A perfect summer salad.

250g instant couscous
5 tbsp olive oil
1/3-1/2 a cucumber
3 ripe tomatoes
2 tsp basil or coriander paste
2-3 tbsp lemon juice
Salt and pepper
2 heaped tbsp finely chopped
   fresh mint leaves
2 heaped tbsp chopped
   coriander or parsley
1/2 small red onion, peeled
   and finely chopped

Make up the couscous following the instructions on the pack, adding 1 tablespoon of the olive oil to the water. Leave it to cool in a large bowl, forking it through to break up any lumps. Cut the cucumber into four lengthways, cut away the seeds and chop into small pieces. Skin and de-seed the tomatoes (*see* p33) and chop finely. Mix together the basil or coriander paste, 2 tablespoons of the lemon juice and the remaining oil and season to taste with salt and pepper. Tip the chopped vegetables and herbs into the couscous, pour over the dressing and toss together thoroughly. Check the seasoning, adding more salt, pepper or lemon juice to taste.

You could also add/substitute

- A handful of black olives.
- 150g cooked fresh or defrosted frozen prawns.
- Some crumbled white cheese (like Feta, Caerphilly or Wensleydale).
- Some strips of cooked or barbecued chicken.
- Cooked peas, broad beans and/or asparagus.
- Or replace the cucumber with chopped chargrilled peppers or courgettes (a couscous salad is a great receptacle for leftovers from the barbecue).

- Herb pastes are quite expensive but useful for quickly zipping up a dressing or pasta sauce.

For sheer value and convenience it's hard to beat a can of beans (the title of this book notwithstanding) but they do need tarting up to make them interesting. There are also times when it's worth cooking them from scratch. This is one of them.

BLACK BEAN CHILLI
V Ve Serves 4

It's a toss-up whether this is a favourite or a feast but it's so popular I've gone for the favourites section. You can make it more elaborate by increasing the number of accompaniments below. Remember: you will need to soak the beans the day before – or make it with canned beans.

250g pack dried black beans or, if you want to speed up the whole process 2 x 400g cans black beans, borlotti beans or red kidney beans
1 green pepper (optional)
3 tbsp sunflower or olive oil
2 medium onions, peeled and thinly sliced
2 large cloves of garlic, peeled and roughly chopped
2 level tsp mild chilli powder
1/2 rounded tsp cumin powder (optional)
1 400g tin whole or chopped tomatoes
Salt
3 heaped tbsp fresh coriander

Soak the beans overnight. Put them on to cook following the instructions on the pack. Meanwhile wash the pepper, cut into quarters, cut away the white pith and seeds and cut into chunks. Heat the oil in a large saucepan, add the onion and pepper and cook for about 7-8 minutes until beginning to soften. Add the chopped garlic, the chilli powder and cumin if using, stir, cook for a minute then add the tomatoes and stir again. Turn the heat down, cover and leave to simmer slowly while the beans carry on cooking. (Or for about 15 minutes if using canned beans.) Drain the beans, add to the tomato mixture, stir, replace the lid and cook for another 10-15 minutes to let the flavours amalgamate. Just before serving check the seasoning, adding salt to taste and stir in the fresh coriander.

Serve with as many of the following as you have time to prepare or can afford. For a feast, lay each out in a bowl.

- A small carton of sour cream.
- 1-2 avocados, peeled, stoned and coarsely chopped.
- 1/2 small pack (about 125g) crumbled white cheese (such as Caerphilly, Cheshire or Wensleydale) or – and this would certainly put it into the feast category – goats cheese.
- A pack of tortilla chips.
- A medium-sized red onion, peeled and roughly chopped.
- Baked sweet potatoes (see p70).

- Any cold leftover beans are really good as a filing for a pitta bread or a wrap.

RED BEAN AND FEATA SALAD ♦ Serves 4

A can of beans – or two – also makes an incredibly quick, easy salad.

2 x 400g red kidney beans or 250g dried red kidney beans, soaked and cooked (following the instructions on the pack)
4 spring onions or 1/2 small red onion, peeled and finely chopped
Double the quantity of the Italian-Style Oil, Lemon and Parsley Dressing (see p56)
200g pack of Feta or Caerphilly or Wensleydale cheese

Tip the beans into a sieve or colander and rinse well under the cold tap. Shake off the excess water and put in a bowl. Trim and finely slice the onions, cut the cheese up into small cubes and add to the salad. Make the dressing, pour over the salad and toss everything well together. Nice with warm pitta bread.

! If you're cooking red kidney beans from scratch it's important to boil them fast for 10 minutes otherwise they can make you ill.

- *See also* Chorizo and Butter Bean Stew p97.

These two recipes came about on separate occasions, then I realised they both relied on the highly successful combination of green beans and new potatoes. Obviously it's best to make them in spring and summer when both vegetables are cheap.

GENOESE PASTA WITH PESTO, POTATOES AND BEANS 🍁 Serves 4

The big advantage of this dish is that you can cook it in one big saucepan – and I do mean big. You want plenty of water so that everything cooks at the same time.

450g new potatoes
Salt and freshly ground pepper
250g dried pasta such as rigatoni
    or penne (not quick-cook)
250g fine green beans
190g jar green pesto – or, even
    better if you can find it on
    special offer, fresh pesto
Freshly grated Parmesan

Wash and scrub the potatoes if you need to. Cut them into halves or quarters so they're all roughly the same size. Cut off the stalk and the curly bit at the end of the beans, unless they are already trimmed, cut them in half and rinse them. Bring a large pan of water to the boil (it's easiest to boil up a couple of kettles), then once it's boiling add about ¹/₂ teaspoon of salt and chuck in the potatoes and pasta. Give them a stir, bring the water back to the boil, cook for about 3 minutes then add the beans. Stir, return the water to the boil then cook for another 10-15 minutes until the potatoes, pasta and beans are tender (take a couple of bits out and see if you can easily stick a knife through them). Meanwhile spoon about three quarters of the pesto into a bowl (about 5 tablespoons). Spoon off 5 tablespoons of the cooking water and mix with the pesto to make a sloppy sauce. Drain the pasta, saving a little more of the cooking water, return to the pan and stir in the pesto sauce and some freshly ground pepper. Taste, adding a little more pesto and water if you feel it needs it. Serve with freshly grated Parmesan.

• If you want to jazz this up a bit you could stir in 250g cherry tomatoes, fried in a little olive oil until soft.

NEW POTATO AND GREEN BEAN BALTI 🍃

Serves 4-6

I say balti but you could use almost any medium hot tomatoey curry sauce – like a tikka masala for instance. Just wait for a special offer.

1kg new potatoes, prepared as in previous recipe
Salt
500g fine green beans, prepared as in previous recipe
1 large (540g) jar good quality balti sauce (e.g. Patak's)
1-2 cloves of garlic, peeled and crushed
1/2 lemon
1/2 large bunch or a small pack of coriander, washed, trimmed and roughly chopped
1/3 large carton of plain low-fat yoghurt

Bring a large pan of water to the boil (see previous recipe) add the potatoes and 1/2 teaspoon of salt, bring back to the boil, cook for 3 minutes then add the beans. Cook for another 8-10 minutes until the potatoes and beans are tender. Meanwhile pour the balti sauce into a pan, add the crushed garlic and heat gently. Spoon off a little of the water you're using to boil the potatoes and beans (about 4-5 tbsp) and add to the sauce together with the juice of half a lemon. Cut the leaves off the coriander and chop roughly. Add about two thirds of the coriander to the sauce. Drain the potatoes and beans. Spoon some of each into individual soup bowls, top with the balti sauce and a good dollop of yoghurt and sprinkle on some more coriander.

• You could use broccoli in this recipe instead of beans if you prefer though microwave or steam it (for about 3-4 minutes) rather than boiling it.

FEASTS

There's really nothing as nice as sharing a meal with your mates. In an ideal world that would be at a restaurant so you don't have to shop, cook or wash up. But eating at home is a lot cheaper and often a lot better than the kind of food you get offered for £10 a head if you go out.

The key to making it enjoyable rather than a tense angst-ridden experience is sharing the load. Which is basically what happens in any restaurant kitchen where there's always someone to chop up veg or make desserts while the chef gets on with the main courses.

The other key to success is acquiring the art of cheating – tarting things up so they look great with minimum effort on your part. From instant curries to sexed-up rice pudding and jelly here are plenty of ingenious ideas.

There's something ultra-comforting about cooking a proper Sunday lunch (or dinner), particularly when you first get to university and are missing home. But if you've never attempted a roast before this is a good recipe to start with.

NO-CARVE ROAST CHICKEN DINNER WITH SAUSAGES, BACON AND CRUNCHY ROAST POTATOES Serves 4-6

This is exactly the same as roasting a whole chicken other than the fact that you don't have to carve it. If you only have one roasting dish, serve boiled potatoes instead or make the wokked roast potatoes below.

1.25 kg potatoes
Salt and pepper
6 tbsp olive oil or
 vegetable/sunflower/rapeseed
 and olive oil mixed
1 kg chicken thighs and
 drumsticks or chicken legs,
 free-range if possible
1/2 tsp dried oregano or thyme
 (optional)
8 streaky bacon rashers
4 cloves of garlic (optional)
400-454g pack of good quality
 sausages
2 tbsp (30g) soft butter
2 tbsp plain flour
2 tsp Marmite

Preheat the oven to 200°C/400°F/Gas 6. Peel the potatoes, halve or quarter depending how big they are and place in a large saucepan. Cover with cold water and bring to the boil (about 5 minutes). Add a little salt and boil for 5 minutes, then strain the potatoes in a colander or sieve, saving 450ml of the cooking water for the gravy. Put 4 tablespoons of oil into a roasting tin and tip in the potatoes, turning them in the oil. Pour the remaining oil into another tin then put in the chicken pieces. Turn them in the oil and season with salt, pepper and a little thyme. Put both the tins in the oven and cook for 30 minutes. Cut the rind off the bacon rashers if necessary then stretch each rasher by running the blunt edge of the knife along the rasher. When 30 minutes is up take out the tin with the chicken, turn over the chicken pieces and season them on the other side.

Add the garlic cloves, sausages and arrange the bacon rashers over the top. Replace the tin in the oven, take out the potato tin and turn the potatoes too. Put them back in the oven and continue to cook while you make the gravy following the recipe for Amazing Marmite Gravy (*see* p78), using the reserved potato water to dissolve the Marmite. Leave it to cook over a very low heat. After another 15 minutes turn over the sausages, turn the heat up to 220°C/425°F/Gas 7 and continue to cook until the potatoes, chicken and bacon are crisp (about another 15 minutes). Cook whatever veg you're serving in the meantime (frozen peas would be fine).

WOKKED ROAST POTATOES 🍁

This has something of the appeal of a deep-fried Mars bar but is hugely effective.

Take ¹/₂ pack (about 450g) frozen roast potatoes and microwave them on high for 3-4 minutes until you can stick a knife through them. Blot them with kitchen towel then fry them in either a wok or a heavy-based frying pan in a couple of centimetres of hot oil, turning them regularly till they're crisp all over. Scoop them out onto a couple of sheets of kitchen towel to blot up the excess fat. (Well, you don't want a coronary, do you?) Sprinkle with salt. Should serve four though my younger son can demolish the lot in one sitting.

- *See also* Baked Chicken with Garlic and Lovely Lemony Potatoes, p104.

A PROPER ROAST CHICKEN DINNER

Serves 4

If you think a roast dinner's not a roast dinner unless you have a large piece of meat sitting in front of you waiting to be carved this is the way to do it. I don't really advocate buying frozen chicken but if you do make sure you defrost it thoroughly at room temperature for at least 12 hours or overnight.

THE CHICKEN

A medium-sized chicken
  (about 1.5kg)
A whole lemon or a handful
  of parsley
Olive oil or sunflower oil
Salt and pepper

Preheat the oven to 200°C/400°F/Gas 6. Remove any giblets from inside the bird (usually tucked in a plastic bag) and stuff it with a lemon or a handful of parsley. Smear the chicken with oil, season with salt and pepper and place it in a roasting tin, breast side upwards. Roast for 20-25 minutes until the breast begins to brown then turn it on one side and roast for another 20 minutes. Holding the chicken, carefully pour or spoon out most of the fat that has accumulated in the pan, then turn the chicken on its other side and cook for another 20 minutes. If it seems to be cooking too quickly turn down the oven a setting and cover it loosely with a sheet of foil. Finally turn it breast side upwards again and give it a final 20 minutes. To test if it's cooked stick a sharp knife into the thickest part of the chicken leg. When you withdraw it any juices that emerge should run clear. Take the chicken out of the oven and let it stand, lightly covered with foil for 10 minutes before you carve it. Meanwhile make the gravy and finish cooking the veg.

- If you've got more than four to feed it's actually easier to cook two smaller chickens side by side than one really big one.

How to carve a chicken

This is a much easier method than attempting to cut neat slices. Cut down either side of the bird and remove the two legs then cut each leg into two pieces – the thigh and drumstick. Run your knife along the left-hand side of the breastbone and loosen the chicken breast away from the carcass. Cut it away in one piece then cut it in half. Repeat with the right hand breast. Cut off the two chicken wings. That's it.

THE GRAVY

Chicken doesn't cook long enough to leave the gorgeous sticky pan residues that pork, lamb or beef do so you need to fiddle about a bit to get a good gravy (unless you decide to opt out altogether and make the Amazing Marmite Gravy, p78).

To make a thin French-style gravy (this won't make huge quantities) pour off the excess fat from the dish, put it on the hob over a low heat and pour in a large glass of white wine or cider. Work the wine round the dish scraping off whatever sticky bits you can prise off the sides then bubble it up and reduce the volume by half. Check the seasoning, adding salt and pepper to taste and stir in a spoonful of double cream or crème fraîche if you like.

For classic English gravy leave a little of the fat in the pan and stir in a tablespoon of flour. Cook for a minute then pour in 250ml of the water in which you've cooked the potatoes or chicken stock or stock made with a teaspoon of Marmite (the latter will make it darker). Bring the gravy to the boil, stirring and scraping off any dark sticky bits from the side of the pan then simmer until thick (about 3-4 minutes). Check the seasoning, adding salt and pepper to taste.

THE POTATOES

There are two good ways of making roast potatoes – the old fashioned British way of boiling them for five minutes first then draining them (saving the water for gravy), tossing them in oil (or if you want to be totally unreconstructed, lard) and roasting them in a hot oven. This is the method I've used for the No-Carve Roast Chicken Dinner (see p128).

The other, slightly quicker way is to peel and cut them in smaller pieces and tip them straight into a roasting pan with 3-4 tablespoons of olive oil, some garlic cloves and rosemary or thyme, like the roast vegetables on p32. Either way you should turn them a couple of times to ensure they brown evenly – they should take about an hour in total so start them off about 15 minutes after you put the chicken in. If they're not cooked by the time the chicken is ready, take the chicken out, turn up the oven and give them a final blast at 220°C/425°F/Gas 7. Season them with a little salt before you serve them.

! In gas ovens the top of the oven is hotter than the bottom, so always cook your potatoes on the top shelf.

THE VEG

Basically it's just a question of choosing which veg you fancy and remembering to cook them in time. Start them about 15 minutes before the chicken is cooked, (see How To Cook Veg, p30). Personally I like peas, green beans or sprouts with roast chicken. Don't be too ambitious – one should be enough.

Why anyone should want to eat more than one Christmas dinner beats me but I know there are plenty who do. Here's how to do it for 6 to 8 people.

THE TURKEY

There's nothing particularly tricky about cooking a turkey. It's just like roasting a chicken except it takes about four times longer. The important thing is to get it cooked right through. There's nothing nastier (or more dangerous) than a turkey with a nicely browned skin and raw meat inside (see earlier comments about defrosting. Allow 24 hours for a turkey.)

The best way is to start it off with a good blast of heat – 20 minutes at 220°C/425°F/Gas 7. Then turn the heat down to 190°C/375°F/Gas 5 and continue to cook it for about 20 minutes per 500g.
A 4.5-5kg bird (enough to feed 6-8 generously) will take about 4 hours in total, maybe more. At some stage you'll need to stop it browning too much (especially the legs and wings) by wrapping them in foil. Spoon off some of the fat that accumulates in the pan otherwise it'll make it hard to crisp your potatoes.
If you don't have room to cook potatoes anyway, boil them for 10 minutes instead of the 5 minutes described on p131, then leave them till you take the turkey out. Turn the oven back up to 220°C again then roast them for 20-25 minutes. The turkey will be fine if you cover it loosely with foil.
Check the turkey carefully before you take it out of the oven. Stick a knife in the thickest part of the leg and see if the juices run clear. If in doubt give it another 10-15 minutes.

! Don't buy too big a turkey otherwise you'll be cooking it all day.

A REALLY GOOD STUFFING (AS IT WERE)

Stuffing the bird itself is not a great idea a) because it absorbs all the fat b) makes it harder to ensure the turkey is properly cooked c) is a pain to do anyway. I would either buy a ready-made (chilled not packet) stuffing and bake it separately or fry up a pan of some of those Christmassy sausages you can buy in most supermarkets. However, if stuffing is the only point of Christmas dinner so far as you're concerned this is a classic.

A 454g pack of sausagemeat or traditional English sausages (e.g. Cumberland)
About 3-4 tbsp dried natural breadcrumbs (not the bright orange ones)
1 large egg, beaten
1/2 small onion (50g) peeled and finely chopped
1 small flavourful apple (e.g. Blenheim or Cox), peeled, quartered, cored and finely chopped
100g ready-to-eat prunes, finely chopped (easiest with scissors)

1 tsp ground mixed spice
Salt and pepper
1 tsp oil

Put the sausagemeat in a bowl with the breadcrumbs and the beaten egg and mix thoroughly together (if you're using sausages, slit the skins and pull them off). Leave while you prepare the rest of the ingredients then mix them in too. Heat the oil in a small to medium size non-stick frying pan and tip in the stuffing. Pat it down with a wooden spoon or fork until it resembles a cake then let it cook for about 5 minutes, covered with a lid or foil. Turn the stuffing over. (Don't worry if it breaks up, just mash it together again.) Continue cooking for another 5-6 minutes till the stuffing is cooked.

THE GRAVY

The good news about all that long slow cooking is that you get some really dark sticky meaty juices in the pan which should make loads of gravy. Carefully pour off most of the fat from the roastng tin into a bowl, leaving the juices behind then stir in 2-3 tablespoons of flour (enough to make a thickish paste). Cook for a minute then gradually stir in about 500ml of potato water or stock made with vegetable bouillon powder, bring to the boil and simmer for 5 minutes. Adjust the seasoning, adding salt and pepper and strain.

THE VEG

Roast potatoes, obviously (see p131) and sprouts. Here's how to tart up frozen ones.

HOT BUTTERED SPROUTS WITH ALMONDS 🥬

Take about 700g of frozen sprouts and plunge them into a large saucepan of boiling, salted water. Cook for about 2 minutes less than they recommend on the pack (as soon as you can stick a sharp knife right through them they're done). Drain them thoroughly in a colander.

Meanwhile rinse and dry the pan and add a good lump (25g) of butter. Melt it over a moderate heat then tip in about a quarter of a small pack (about 25g) of flaked almonds. Stir them around then when they start to brown return the sprouts to the pan and toss with the butter and almonds. Season generously with freshly ground pepper.

CHEAT'S CHRISTMAS PUDDING 🥬 Serves 8

Unbelievably easy, and a bit lighter on the stomach than the traditional pud.

2 tubs of good quality vanilla ice-cream (Haagen Daaz as it's Christmas)
A 400g jar of mincemeat
A 5cl miniature of of brandy or whisky or a good slosh of sherry

Scoop the mincemeat into a small saucepan and add the brandy, whisky or sherry. Heat slowly, stirring, and pour over the ice-cream.

Shoulder of lamb goes amazingly well with either the bean or the potato recipe that follows. If you're not much into garlic, cutting the quantities down won't do any harm. Warm Plum and Rum Tart (see p138) makes a great pud to follow this lamb dish.

ROAST LAMB WITH ROSEMARY AND GARLIC RUB Serves 4-6

Shoulder of lamb is surprisingly affordable, especially New Zealand lamb.

A 1.5-1.6kg shoulder of lamb
 or 2 half shoulders
 (which can be cheaper)
1 rounded tsp coarse or fine
 sea salt
2 large cloves of garlic, peeled
 and roughly chopped
1 rounded tsp black
 peppercorns
1½ tsp dried rosemary, thyme
 or herbes de Provence
2 tbsp olive oil
1 large (175ml) glass white
 or red wine (optional)

Smash the salt, garlic, herbs and peppercorns together Jamie-style with a pestle and mortar or in a bowl with the end of a rolling pin. Add 2 tablespoons of olive oil and mix thoroughly. Trim any large chunks of fat off the meat with a sharp knife, make some random deep cuts in the meat and rub the marinade thoroughly into the meat. If you have time leave it covered at room temperature for an hour. Heat the oven to 190°C/375°F/Gas 5. Place the meat in a roasting tin and add a small glass of water. Roast it for about 1¾-2 hours, taking it out every half-hour or so to spoon or pour off some of the excess fat, spoon some of the pan juices over the meat and add extra water if needed. Half an hour before you think the meat should be ready pour in the wine (if using) instead of the water. When the meat is cooked take it out and put it on a plate or chopping board and cover lightly with foil. Carefully pour off the rest of the fat from the tin, leaving the dark sticky juices behind then pour 250ml of water into the tin and work it around with a wooden spoon. Heat the gravy through, then taste it. If it seems a bit sharp add a teaspoon of tomato ketchup or tomato paste or a little butter. If it's a bit bland season with salt and pepper or add a teaspoon of lemon juice or wine vinegar. Cut the meat into rough chunks and serve with the gravy.

• If you have neither a pestle and mortar nor rolling pin, you can always insert fine slices of garlic into the holes you make in the meat, season it with salt, pepper and herbs (rub them between your fingers to break them down and pour over the olive oil).

CREAMY BEANS WITH GARLIC 🍁 🍁 Serves 4-6

Amazingly these beans don't actually have cream in them, they just become creamy through simmering and energetic stirring.

2 x 400g cans of flageolet
  or cannellini beans
3 tbsp olive oil
2 cloves of garlic, crushed
  or finely chopped
1 tsp dried thyme
Salt and freshly ground black
  pepper

Drain the beans in a sieve or colander and rinse well. Put them in a saucepan with the oil, garlic and thyme and add a small glass of water.

Heat slowly, stirring vigorously then leave to simmer, stirring occasionally, until the water has been absorbed. Add more water, stir, cook and stir again. Repeat a couple more times, adding extra water until the beans are soft and creamy (takes about 12-15 minutes in all). Season to taste with a little salt and plenty of pepper.

• These also go really well with sausages.

CREAMY GARLIC AND POTATO BAKE 🍁
Serves 6

So good you could eat it on its own.

284 ml carton whipping cream
2 cloves of garlic, peeled and
  cut into thin slices
750g potatoes
25g soft butter plus a bit extra
  for buttering the dish
Salt and pepper
100ml semi-skimmed milk
2 tbsp fresh Parmesan

Heat the oven to 190°C/375°F/Gas 5. Pour the cream into a small saucepan and heat very gently with the sliced garlic. Leave to infuse off the heat while you peel the potatoes and cut them into very thin slices. Butter a shallow ovenproof dish and place a layer of potatoes over the bottom. Dot a bit of butter on the potato and season with salt and pepper. Repeat until all the potatoes are used. Pour over the warm cream and enough milk to come almost to the top of the potatoes. Sprinkle over the grated Parmesan and bake for 50-60 minutes until the top is browned and the potatoes cooked through.

Here are two veggie lunches that meat-eaters will definitely want to share. Says it all, really.

SPICED SWEET POTATO, PEPPER AND AUBERGINE BAKE ✿
Serves 6

You can of course vary the veg depending on what's available though I like this combination.

2 medium to large onions
  (about 350g)
6 tbsp olive or sunflower oil
2-3 sweet potatoes
  (about 450g), peeled and
  cut into large cubes
1 medium to large aubergine
  (about 350g), cut into large
  cubes
1 large red or green pepper
  (about 175g), cut into large
  chunks
250g okra (optional)
2 large cloves of garlic
1 tbsp Moroccan Spice Mix
  (*see* p35)
400g can of chopped tomatoes
250 ml stock made with 1 tsp
  Marigold vegetable bouillon
  powder
Salt, sugar and Tabasco or hot
  pepper sauce to taste
400g can of chickpeas, drained
  and rinsed
3 heaped tbsp fresh coriander
  leaves, roughly chopped
1 small carton of sour cream

Preheat the oven to 200°C/400°F/ Gas 6. Peel one of the onions and cut into eight. Pour 4 tablespoons of the oil in a large roasting tin. Add the onion, cubed sweet potatoes, aubergine and pepper, mix well with the oil and bake in the oven for 30 minutes, turning them half way through. Meanwhile peel and roughly chop the other onion and prepare the okra if using (see below). Heat the remaining 2 tablespoons of the oil in a large frying pan and fry the onion and okra gently for about 10 minutes. Add the garlic and spices and stir well. Add the chopped tomatoes and cook for about 5 minutes. Stir in the stock then check the seasoning adding salt and a pinch of sugar to taste.

Add a dash of chilli sauce or Tabasco if you don't think it's hot enough. Lastly add the chickpeas. When the vegetables in the oven have been cooking for 30 minutes pour over the spiced tomato mixture and stir in well. Turn the oven temperature down to 190°C/375°F/Gas 5 and cook for another 20-30 minutes until the vegetables are well cooked, turning them half way through. Just before serving add the chopped coriander. Serve each portion with a dollop of sour cream.

- Okra is an Indian vegetable with a distinctive almost lemony flavour. You can buy it cheapest in Asian grocers. Wash and trim the stalks off before using.

CHILEAN CORN PIE ♥
Serves 6

This style of corn-topped pie is popular in various parts of South America, normally made with chicken or beef. This lighter vegetarian version can be made with Quorn or soy mince. You'll need some kind of a blender for the topping.

2 tbsp olive oil
2 medium onions (about 250g), peeled and finely chopped
1-2 cloves of garlic, peeled and crushed
1 rounded tbsp tomato paste (optional)
1 400g tin chopped tomatoes or 250g passata
350g pack minced Quorn or soy mince
1/2 level tsp ground cinnamon or mixed spice
1 small tin pimento stuffed olives (about 75g drained weight), roughly chopped
3 heaped tbsp chopped parsley
Salt and pepper

For the corn topping
500g frozen corn or 2 x 326g tins of sweetcorn without added sugar or salt
1 250g carton of Quark or a 200g carton of fromage frais
4 medium or 3 large eggs, lightly beaten
Salt and pepper

Heat the olive oil over a moderate heat in a large frying pan, add the onion and cook gently for about 6-7 minutes until soft. Add the crushed garlic and tomato paste, stir and cook for another minute. Add the chopped tomatoes or passata, stir well then add the Quorn. Mix together thoroughly then add the chopped olives. Cook for another five minutes then add the parsley and season with salt and pepper. Set aside. If you're using frozen corn cook it in boiling water for 3 minutes, drain then rinse in cold water. Whizz together in a blender or food processor with the Quark or fromage frais then gradually add the beaten eggs. Season generously with salt and pepper.

Tip the Quorn mixture into a shallow greased ovenproof dish, top with the corn mixture and spread it evenly over the mince. Bake in a pre-heated oven at 190°C/375°F/Gas 5 for about 30 minutes until the top is lightly set. Serve with a large green salad or stir-fried greens.

- You could also make this with 450g minced pork or beef.
- Olives stuffed with pimento are quite a bit cheaper than ones which are marinated in herbs and garlic. They're not wildly exciting on their own but are a good addition to tomatoey sauces and stews.

A tart and a crumble: two classic Sunday lunch puds – one British, one French.

WARM PLUM AND RUM TART ✿ Serves 6

Ready-rolled pastry makes it possible to run up a flashy-looking tart in no time. All you have to do is score the pastry so the edge rises up either side of the fruit. Keep it in the fridge and put it on to cook just before you dish up the main course.

A large punnet (about 700g) plums
2 tbsp rum or vodka
5-6 tbsp (preferably unrefined) caster or granulated sugar
230g pack of ready-rolled puff pastry
25g butter straight from the fridge
1 beaten egg

Wash the plums and cut vertically round the stone. Holding one side of the fruit in each hand twist them in different directions so the two halves come apart. Pull away the stone and cut the halves into half again. Put the plum quarters into a bowl with the rum and 2 tablespoons of sugar and mix well. Leave until you want to make the tart, stirring them occasionally to make sure they stay rummy.

Take the pastry out of the fridge about 10 minutes before you want to use it and turn the oven on to 220°C/425°F/Gas 7. Unroll the pastry and lay it out on a lightly oiled baking tray or large baking sheet. With a sharp knife score a line 2cm from the edge of your piece of pastry without cutting right the way through it. Brush this outside edge with beaten egg taking care not to brush over the line, then sprinkle the middle with 1-2 tablespoons of sugar (depending how ripe the plums are). Arrange the plums round the tart, making sure they don't overlap the line you've made. Sprinkle on another 1-2 tablespoons of sugar then cut little flakes off the butter and dot them around the top. Place the baking tray in the oven and bake for about 15-20 minutes till the pastry is well risen and the fruit is bubbling. Serve with cream or ice cream.

• You can make this tart with other stoned fruit such as peaches or nectarines.

A GOOD OLD-FASHIONED APPLE CRUMBLE

Serves 6

The secret of a really good apple crumble is cooking the fruit before you top it with the crumble mixture. Takes a bit longer but it makes it possible to get your fruit soft and fluffy and your topping nice and crunchy.

3-4 medium to large Bramley apples (about 900g)
¼ tsp ground cinnamon (optional)
4 tbsp caster sugar (preferably unrefined)
2 tbsp soft butter (about 25g)

For the crumble topping
175g plain flour
110g butter at fridge temperature
50g unrefined caster sugar

Peel, quarter and cut out the core from the apples and slice them thickly into a large saucepan. Sprinkle with the cinnamon, 3 tablespoons of the sugar, add half the butter and pour over 3 tablespoons of water. Cover the pan, place over a low heat and cook for about 12-15 minutes, shaking the pan occasionally until the apple pieces are soft but still holding their shape. Tip them into a medium-sized shallow ovenproof dish and leave them to cool. Measure the flour into a large bowl. Cut the butter into small cubes and tip into the flour. Keep cutting until you can't get the pieces of butter any smaller then rub the butter and flour together with the tips of your fingers, lifting it up and letting it fall back again into the bowl. Do this until the mixture is the consistency of coarse breadcrumbs. Stir in the sugar and carry on rubbing for another minute. (You can do this in seconds in a food processor.) When the apples have cooled down turn the oven to 200°C/ 400°F/Gas 6.

Spread the crumble mixture evenly over the apples making sure you cover the whole surface, then bake for about 30-40 minutes till the crumble is brown and the fruit juices bubbling along the sides of the dish. Serve with cream, vanilla ice-cream or ready-made chilled custard.

- If you're making a crumble to go with a roast put it in when you take the meat and potatoes out of the oven.
- To make a slightly fancier crumble add 125g fresh or frozen blackberries or a handful of raisins to the apples and/or replace 50g of the flour with finely chopped walnuts.
- Other fruits that work well in crumbles include those mixed bags of frozen summer fruits, rhubarb, apricots or plums (stone them first). You need slightly less than you do apples – about 700g.

It might seem odd putting a section on barbecues in a student cookbook but if there's any space to set one up at the back of your house, chances are you're going to be out there lighting up. Even if you haven't one these recipes are great for summer eating.

Which barbie to buy?

Basic barbecues are really cheap (everyone wants those flashy gas jobs). You can buy one for for as little as £10 though you'll probably need to spend around £15-20 if you want to cook enough for four or six. Disposable barbecues are tempting but expensive, unless they're on special offer, but try them if you're nervous and have never barbecued before.

Which charcoal?

You can either buy lumpwood (which looks like small pieces of coal) or briquettes. Lumpwood burns quicker, briquettes last a bit longer. Unless they're already impregnated with fuel you'll also need some kind of firelighters or lighting fluid (use ones that are designed for barbecues not for ordinary fires).

How to light up

Tip a good layer of charcoal (about 3-4 cm deep) in the base of the barbecue tray then pile it up into a pyramid. Tuck pieces of firelighter around the pile or pour over firelighter fluid following the instructions on the bottle. Light (preferably with a long match) and wait until you can see the coals starting to glow (about 15 minutes). Spread them out and leave them to get really hot (another 30 minutes). Once there are no more flames and the coals are covered with a fine layer of white ash you're ready to cook. (You should be able to hold your hand about 15cm away from the coals for 3-4 seconds.) Brush the cooking rack lightly with oil before you start. Obviously the nearer the rack is to the coals the hotter it will be and the centre of the barbecue will also be hotter than the sides. If it doesn't seem hot enough open any vents in the base of the barbecue, knock some of the ash off the coals and push them closer together. To reduce the heat, close the vents and push the coals apart. You should get about 30-45 minutes cooking time from the original fire. Push some extra coals around the edge of the barbecue to heat up if you want to extend that.

Safety tips

- NEVER pour lighting fluid on a barbecue once it's alight or use anything other than a product designed for barbecues. Don't use aerosol oil sprays on food either once it's cooking.
- Make sure the barbecue is stable. Put it on an even surface away from overhanging branches, fences or anything else that could catch fire.
- Don't cook with floppy sleeves. Use long handled cooking tools (again, quite cheap to buy).
- Don't barbecue if it's windy.
- Once the barbecue is alight someone should stay with it. Don't attempt to move it. Make sure it's completely out before you leave it.
- Don't use portable barbecues indoors.

- Have a spray bottle of water handy to dampen down any flare-ups.
- Don't leave raw meat lying around in the hot sun.

What to cook

On an inexpensive barbecue stick to food that is going to cook easily – such as burgers, sausages or kebabs. They should be at room temperature before you start. If you want to cook chicken, part-cook it first – either in a conventional oven, microwave or grill – then finish it off on the barbecue. Vegetables like aubergines, peppers and courgettes also barbecue well but don't cut them too small or they'll fall through the grill. All food needs to be brushed lightly with oil so it doesn't scorch or stick; that is unless it has been marinated (in which case shake off the marinade before cooking or your food will catch fire). You'll also need to turn it at least once during the cooking time, brushing on a little more oil or marinade.

How long it takes...

Burgers Roughly 3-4 minutes each side. Very thin ones might take a bit less.

Sausages Frankfurters (a good option for barbies) take 3-4 minutes. Fatter sausages should be part-cooked like chicken then finished off for 5-6 minutes on the barbecue.

Chicken Use thighs and drumsticks. If you part-cook them for about 10 minutes in a hot oven or under a grill they should only take another 10-15 minutes to cook.

Aubergines, peppers and courgettes About 3-4 minutes each side.

Flat mushrooms About 7-8 minutes (cook with the underside upwards and don't turn them or you'll lose the delicious juices).

Halloumi cheese (a good option for vegetarians) About 3 minutes each side.

How to clean up afterwards

Once you've finished cooking douse the coals with cold water or simply leave the barbecue to die out if there aren't many coals left. Once completely cold tip out the ash and clean any burnt food off the rack with a wire brush, crumpled piece of newspaper or foil. Wipe the rack lightly with oil.

Marinades and salsas are what will make your barbecue edible. Even a bog-standard burger can be improved with a splash of chimichurri salsa (*see* opposite), while a mass-produced chicken that's been marinated in oil and lemon juice can actually taste quite sophisticated. Home-made salsas are much, much nicer than the bottled variety. You need the crunch that only fresh fruit and vegetables can give. You can of course buy these products ready-made but the cheap ones aren't that good and the good ones are pricey.

A SIMPLE OIL AND LEMON MARINADE...

Juice of 2 lemons
   (about 5-6 tbsp)
4 tbsp olive oil
2 cloves of garlic, crushed
A couple of sprigs of fresh thyme or rosemary or $1/2$ tsp dried oregano, thyme or herbes de Provence

Whisk the oil and lemon juice together in a shallow ovenproof dish with 2 tablespoons of water, the garlic and herbs.

• This will make enough for 1kg of chicken pieces (preferably free-range).

• **And how to use it....**
   It's up to you whether you skin the chicken or not. Either way, stab the fleshy parts of the meat a few times to help the marinade penetrate then lay the pieces in a single layer in the marinade. Turn so both sides are coated, cover with cling film and leave in a cool place for 1-2 hours.

Either heat the grill or a moderate oven (190°C/375°F/Gas 5) and cook the chicken pieces for about 10-15 minutes, turning them once. Transfer them to the barbecue, shaking off any excess marinade (which would make the coals flare up) and cook for another 10-15 minutes or until any juices run clear when you stick a sharp knife in them. (Obviously if you haven't a barbecue you can finish the cooking under the grill or in the oven).

• This also works very well on lamb.

TANDOORI MARINADE

2 tbsp tandoori or other
medium-hot curry paste
A small (150ml) carton of plain,
unsweetened yoghurt
1 clove of garlic crushed
1-2 tsp lemon juice

Mix the tandoori paste and
yoghurt together and thin with
a couple of tablespoons of water.
Season with the garlic and a little
lemon juice to taste. Follow the
instructions above for marinading
and cooking the chicken.

- This will make enough for 1kg
  of chicken pieces (preferably
  free-range).

RED-HOT PINEAPPLE SALSA 🍁 🍁

*A great salsa to serve with grilled
or barbecued chicken. Try and
use fresh pineapple if possible.*

About 450g peeled, fresh
pineapple or 2 x 227g tins
of pineapple slices in natural
juice

2 mild green chillies, deseeded
(*see* p35) and very finely
chopped
4-5 tbsp sweet chilli sauce
2-3 tbsp freshly squeezed lime
juice
Salt to taste
3 tbsp chopped coriander leaves

Cut the pineapple into small
chunks and place in a bowl
with 1 tablespoon of its juice.
Add the green chillies, sweet chilli
sauce and lime juice and salt
to taste. Mix well and refrigerate
till needed. Add the chopped
coriander just before serving.

CHIMICHURRI SALSA

Chimichurri is the punchy
parsley, garlic and chilli-based
sauce that Argentinians use as
a standard accompaniment for
steak, but it's just as effective
with burgers which have more
need of rescuing. The salt water
component sounds weird but
it works.

100ml olive oil
50 ml red or white wine vinegar
1 tsp dried oregano or 1/2 tsp
dried thyme
4 tbsp finely chopped fresh
parsley
1/2-1 level tsp crushed red
chillies (depending how hot
you want it)
1 large garlic clove, finely
chopped
1 bay leaf (optional)
100 ml salmuera (a salt water
solution made from 1 level
tbsp sea salt dissolved in
100 ml warm water and cooled)

Mix the ingredients for the
sauce together in a large
screw-top jar, shake well and
refrigerate overnight (important)
for the flavours to infuse. Once
you've cooked the burgers
splash over some of the salsa.

- *See also* Fresh Tomato Salsa,
  and Cucumber and Sweet
  Chilli Salsa, both p64.

Unless you're an unreconstructed carnivore you're going to need a salad to relieve the meat-fest.

It's best to base this on some kind of carbohydrate which will fill everyone up and make the meat stretch further – potatoes, pasta, rice, beans and couscous are all good candidates.

THE ULTIMATE POTATO SALAD 🍁
Serves 8

The Warm Potato and Sausage Salad (see p99) is good. This is sublime.

1 kg new potatoes
4 tbsp light salad dressing made from 1 tbsp wine vinegar whisked with 3 tbsp sunflower oil or light olive oil, seasoned with a little salt and pepper
5-6 spring onions, trimmed and finely sliced or 1 small red onion, peeled and finely chopped
1 large or 2 medium pickled sweet-sour cucumbers
3 large hard boiled eggs (optional)
2 heaped tbsp low-fat mayonnaise
1 heaped tbsp low-fat crème fraîche
2 tbsp each finely chopped dill and flat leaf parsley or 4 tbsp finely chopped parsley
Salt and ground black pepper

Cut the potatoes into even-sized pieces leaving the smaller potatoes whole and put into a saucepan. Cover them with boiling water, bring them to the boil, add a little salt and simmer for 15 minutes until just cooked. Drain them in a colander, spreading them out so they cool quickly. As soon as they are cool enough to handle (about 8-10 minutes) cut each piece into 2-3 pieces. Transfer to a mixing bowl and pour over the salad dressing and the chopped spring onions. Turn the potatoes in the dressing taking care not to break them up. Meanwhile finely chop the pickled cucumbers, hard boiled eggs and herbs. Spoon the mayonnaise and crème fraîche into a small bowl, mix well, thin with 3-4 teaspoons of liquid from the pickled cucumber jar and season with pepper. Once the potatoes are cool add the rest of the ingredients holding back about a third of the egg and the herbs. Mix together lightly but thoroughly.

Check the seasoning adding more pepper and a little salt if you think it needs it. Transfer to a clean serving bowl (if you have one) and sprinkle the remaining egg and chopped herbs over the surface.

- This is also really good with ham and other cold meats.
- You could also make the Red Bean and Feta Salad ·(see p123) or the Cucumber, Herb or Couscous Salad (see p121).

SALMON, SUGARSNAP PEA AND PASTA SALAD Serves 4-6

This is admittedly rather an elaborate salad to serve with a barbecue so look at it more as an alternative for those who are not burger and banger fans. It's really good anyway.

300g cooked pasta shapes (100g dried)
I small (150g) pack sugarsnap peas or mange-tout
1 large can (418g) of red salmon (preferably Alaskan) or 2 microwaved or steamed boneless salmon fillets (250-300g)
2 tbsp low-fat mayonnaise
2 tbsp low-fat crème fraîche
Salt and pepper
1-2 tbsp lemon juice
A few chives or finely sliced spring onions (optional)

If you don't have any cooked pasta cook it first following the instructions on the pack, drain it then rinse it in cold water.

Microwave or boil the sugarsnap peas for 1-2 minutes until just cooked but still crunchy. Drain and rinse in cold water. Carefully drain and flake the salmon removing any bones and dark bits of skin. Mix the mayonnaise and crème fraîche in a large bowl and season with salt, pepper and lemon juice to taste. Add the pasta and sugarsnap peas and mix well, then add the salmon carefully without breaking it up too much. Serve sprinkled with some chopped chives or very finely sliced spring onions.

- In early summer you may actually be able to make this more cheaply with fresh salmon and asparagus rather than sugarsnap peas. Look out for the very thin asparagus called sprue. You can use the stalks as well as the tips. Microwave or steam them (for about 4 minutes) then let them cool down before you make the salad.

However well organised you are about your barbecue, chances are it will take longer than you imagine and everyone will be starving before you've started to cook the first sausage. This is where a couple of dips or spreads come in handy, not to mention that perennial favourite, garlic bread.

CHEAT'S HUMMUS

V Serves 6-8

I always serve hummus to give vegetarians something substantial to eat with their barbecued veg (assuming everyone else hasn't scoffed it first). Basing it on a can is cheaper than buying it chilled.

1 rounded tsp dry-roasted cumin seeds (optional but good)
A 400g can of hummus (the Cypressa brand is good)
2 tbsp plain low-fat yoghurt
Freshly ground black pepper, salt and lemon juice to taste
1 clove of garlic, peeled, chopped and crushed with a little salt or 1 tsp garlic paste
2 packs of pitta bread to serve

Put the cumin seeds into a small frying pan and heat over a low heat for about 5 minutes until they start to smell aromatic and go dark brown. Take off the heat and cool. Tip the hummus into a large bowl and mash till smooth. Mix in the yoghurt and season with garlic, lemon juice and pepper to taste. Stir in the roasted cumin seeds. Warm the pitta breads under a moderate grill (or two by two on a low setting in a toaster). When toasted, cut them into strips and pile them up on a plate covered with a tea-towel to keep them warm. Serve with some garlicky olives.

- To crush garlic with salt, pound it in a pestle and mortar or in a cup with the back of a teaspoon. It reduces the raw garlic taste and is smoother for a dip.
- Dry-roasting cumin makes it more aromatic (see p35).

AUTHENTIC ROUGH-CRUSHED GUACAMOLE **V** **V8**

Serves 6-8

This is not only easier than having to put everything in a blender – it's the way they do it in Mexico. And it's a lot nicer too.

3 ripe medium-sized avocados
Juice of a lime (2 tbsp)
1/2 white or red onion (about 75g) finely chopped
1 small green chilli, deseeded and finely chopped (see p35)
1 large clove of garlic, peeled and crushed with 1/4 tsp salt
1 tbsp olive oil
2 tomatoes, skinned, seeded and finely chopped (see p33)
3 tbsp finely chopped fresh coriander

Peel the avocados and scoop their flesh into a large bowl, removing any black bits. Mash with a fork until you have a chunky paste. Pour over the lime juice then add the finely chopped onion, chilli, crushed garlic and olive oil and mix in well. Season with black pepper and extra salt if you think it needs it. Stir in the chopped tomatoes and fresh coriander. Cover and refrigerate until ready to serve (don't make it more than an hour in advance). Good with Fresh Tomato Salsa (*see* p64) and tortilla chips.

GOOD OLD-FASHIONED GARLIC BREAD 🍁
Serves 6-8

This is the kind your parents were brought up on and probably still make at home (if you're lucky).

2 baguettes or French sticks, preferably a day old
125g butter at room temperature
4 cloves of garlic, peeled and crushed
4 tbsp finely chopped parsley (optional)
Salt and pepper

Heat the oven to 200°C/400°F/Gas 6. Cut the bread in thick diagonal slices without cutting right through the loaf (i.e. leave it attached at the base). Mash the butter with a wooden spoon until soft and creamy then add the garlic, seasoning and parsley if using. Spread it generously on either side of the cuts you've made. Wrap the bread in foil and bake for 10 minutes. Loosen the foil and replace in the oven for another 5 minutes to brown and crisp up the top.

QUICK GARLIC FLATBREADS 🍁 Serves 8

This has the major advantage that you don't need to use the oven.

4 thin, fresh pizza bases (look in the pizza section)
125g soft garlic butter, bought ready-made or following the previous recipe

Cut the pizza bases in half and lay them upside down on a foil-lined grill pan (you'll have to do this in batches). Cook under a low to moderate heat for a minute then turn them over and spread them with some of the garlic butter. Put them back under the grill for about 2 minutes until the surface is crisp and the garlic has melted (don't cook them too quickly or they'll burn). Serve straightaway, cut into wedges.

The big advantage of summer is that it's a lot less effort to run up a dessert than it is in the winter. There's strawberries and ice-cream for a start but here are some flashier, more impressive options.

SMASHED STRAWBERRY MERINGUE 🍁 Serves 4-6

This very traditional English pudding is known as Eton Mess. For obvious reasons I think this is a better name for it. This should stretch to 6 but I wouldn't bank on it so double the recipe if you want plenty to go round.

1 large (about 450g) pack of strawberries
1 tbsp caster sugar plus 2 tsp for the cream
1 pack of meringue nests (Marks and Sparks do really good ones that taste just like home-made meringues)
284 ml carton double cream
150 ml carton whipping cream

Pull the stalks off the strawberries and slice them thickly. Save a few slices then sprinkle 1 tablespoon of the sugar over the rest and set aside. Break up the meringues into chunky pieces. Mix the two creams together with the remaining sugar and beat with an electric or handheld whisk until it just about holds its shape. (If you pull the whisk upwards through the cream it should form a floppy peak). Layer up the strawberries, meringue and cream in a bowl (ideally a glass one) finishing with a layer of cream. Chill in the fridge till you're ready to eat it then decorate with the remaining strawberries.

• You can also add random scoops of vanilla ice-cream to this, in which case cut down on the amount of cream and serve it straightaway.

! Don't over-beat cream or it becomes solid and heavy and develops a slightly unpleasant buttery flavour.

LIQUID SUMMER PUDDING 🌱 Serves 4-6

This fantastically easy Danish-inspired summer pudding is a great way to make under-ripe strawberries taste ripe and sweet.

A 250g pack frozen raspberries
About 375g strawberries or
 a mixture of strawberries,
 blackberries and raspberries
3 large dollops (about 175g) soft
 set continental-style raspberry
 jam (like Bonne Maman or an
 own-brand equivalent)

Pull the stalks off the strawberries and slice thickly. Spoon the jam into a saucepan. Add the frozen raspberries and cook over a low heat, stirring occasionally until the raspberries thaw out. Increase the heat slightly until the mixture starts to bubble then take off the heat and add the remaining red fruits. Stir and leave to cool in the fridge, until chilled. Serve with pouring cream (double or whipping cream) or vanilla ice-cream.

! Soft fruit deteriorates quickly so if you buy it cheap check it through for any mouldy berries.

ROAST CINNAMON PEACHES WITH GREEK YOGHURT AND HONEY
🌱 Serves 6-8

You can barbecue fruit just as easily as vegetables though it does help to have a separate rack to lay them on, so they don't fall off or end up tasting of garlic from the marinades you've used.

6-8 medium-sized ripe peaches
 (one per person)
50g butter
1 tbsp unrefined caster sugar
 mixed with 1/2 rounded tsp
 ground cinnamon
1 large carton Greek yoghurt
Some good, preferably Greek,
 runny honey

Run a knife vertically round the outside of each peach, cutting through to the stone. Holding one half of the peach in each hand, twist them in different directions to pull them apart. Cut out the stone if it hasn't come away. Melt the butter gently in a small saucepan or microwave and brush or smear it over the peach halves. Lightly oil a rack and lay the peaches over it, cut-side downwards. Barbecue for about 15 minutes (depending how hot your barbecue is) turning them half way through the cooking time and sprinkling the cinnamon sugar over them. Serve with dollops of Greek yoghurt and honey drizzled over the top.

- If you haven't got enough heat left in the barbecue roast the peaches in a lightly oiled roasting tin at 220°C/425°F/ Gas 7 for 15 minutes, turning them as described above.
- You can also make this with nectarines, apricots or plums.

Unless you're a fanatically keen cook it really makes no sense making a curry from scratch. But there are ways of combining the ready-made and the home-made to keep the costs down, make an impressive looking feast and give the impression you've done it all yourself. Making your own rice makes sense for a start and home-made dhals are a lot nicer – and cheaper – than most ready-made versions. You can also stretch ready-made meals by adding to them (there's never enough chicken, for example in a chicken curry) or making an Indian-inspired accompaniment like a fresh coriander chutney. Here's how to do it.

THAI TOFU, SWEETCORN AND SUGARSNAP PEA CURRY V Ve Serves 4-6

Ready-meals may be pricey but the flavour is infinitely better than most curry sauces – and often better than you get in restaurants. You can always make them go further by adding extra meat or, in this case, veg and tofu, plus as many of the other flavourings as you think it needs.

2 x 400g packs Thai Vegetable Curry (the ones with yellow sauce are good)
A 150g pack of fresh organic tofu, cut into small cubes
A small pack of mixed baby sweetcorn and sugarsnap peas or mange-tout
1-2 cloves of garlic, crushed
1-2 mild green or red chillies, seeded and finely chopped (optional, you may think the curry is hot enough already)
4 fresh lime leaves very finely sliced or 4 dried leaves, soaked in water and finely sliced (optional)
A small chunk of peeled, grated fresh ginger or 1 tsp ginger paste (optional)
1-1$\frac{1}{2}$ tbsp fresh lemon juice
3 heaped tbsp finely chopped coriander

Turn the curry into a saucepan and start to heat up gently. Cut the sweetcorn and mange-tout into three pieces, place in a microwaveable dish, cover with a damp piece of kitchen towel and microwave for 2 minutes. Stand for a minute and drain (or you can steam them). Add the vegetables to the curry, along with the tofu, crushed garlic, chilli, lime leaves and ginger if using, and heat through for 5 minutes. Just before serving the curry adjust the seasoning with lemon juice and stir in the chopped coriander. This goes well with Thai jasmine rice (start cooking it before you make the curry, following the instructions on the pack, then once cooked leave it till the curry is ready.)

KERALAN-STYLE PRAWN CURRY WITH MUSSELS, COCONUT AND CORIANDER

Serves 6

Another inspired cheat, this gives an exotic south Indian spin to a pack of frozen prawns. The result looks seriously impressive.

1 large onion (about 200g), peeled and finely chopped
3 tbsp sunflower or light olive oil
2 cloves of garlic
A chunk of fresh ginger about 2 cm square or 1 tsp ginger paste
2 fresh green chillies
1 tbsp ground coriander
1 tsp turmeric
A pinch of chilli powder or cayenne pepper
Salt to taste
2 ripe tomatoes (about 175g) skinned (see p33) and cut into small dice (optional)
400ml can coconut milk
400g pack of frozen prawns or fresh prawns
400g pack chilled or frozen mussels in garlic butter sauce
2-3 tsp lemon juice
4 heaped tbsp of finely chopped fresh coriander

Finely chop the onion. Heat the oil in a wok or large saucepan and fry the onion until well browned (about 10 minutes). Peel and finely chop the garlic and ginger and deseed and finely chop the chillies. Add to the onion and cook, stirring, for a couple more minutes then add the ground coriander, turmeric, chilli powder and a pinch of salt and cook for a minute more. Add the diced tomatoes and coconut milk, bring to the boil and simmer for 10 minutes until the sauce has thickened slightly. Add the prawns to the curry and heat through for about 10 minutes (5 minutes if they're fresh or have thawed). Microwave or boil the mussels in their bag, following the instructions on the pack, and add to the curry once the prawns are ready. Check the seasoning adding a little more salt if necessary, some lemon juice and half the chopped coriander.

Ladle into soup plates, sprinkle over the remaining coriander. This goes well with fluffy rice (see p114) and/or garlic and coriander naan (see p73) warmed under the grill or in a toaster.

- Almost any ready-made Indian curry or sauce can be improved by a squeeze of lemon, a dollop of plain yoghurt and some chopped fresh coriander or – in the case of Thai curries – coriander, 3-4 finely sliced lime leaves and a squeeze of lime. Garlic lovers may want to add extra garlic too.

Even if you buy in a couple of curries it's worth making your own accompaniments. Rice is easy – follow the fluffy rice method (*see* p114) or make a pilau. But the recipe I could happily eat on its own is a dhal.

TARKA DHAL WITH CRISPY ONIONS v v6

Serves 4-6

Grinding your own spices might seem a slog but really does give a better flavour. If you haven't got a pestle and mortar place them on a piece of foil on a chopping board and crush them with the side of a tin.

250g red lentils
$1/2$ tsp turmeric
A small chunk (about 2cm square) fresh ginger, peeled and coarsely grated
4 tbsp sunflower or grapeseed oil
1 medium onion, peeled and finely sliced
1 tbsp coriander seeds or 2 tsp ground coriander
2 large cloves of garlic, peeled and finely chopped
1 tbsp cumin seeds or 2 tsp ground cumin
A pinch (about $1/4$ tsp) chilli powder or cayenne pepper
$1/2$-1 tsp salt
2 heaped tbsp finely chopped fresh coriander

Put the lentils in a pan with the turmeric, grated ginger and 850ml cold water. Bring to the boil and carefully spoon off any froth on the top. Part-cover the pan and simmer for about 25-30 minutes or until the water is absorbed, (you want it sloppy rather than stiff). Meanwhile, fry the onion in 2 tablespoons of the oil over a medium heat turning regularly until the edges of the slices have turned dark brown (about 10 minutes). Remove from the pan. Crush the coriander seeds (*see* above). Heat the remaining oil, fry the garlic for a minute then add the crushed coriander, cumin seeds and chilli powder. Cook for another minute then return the onions to the pan and heat through. Season the dhal with salt to taste and stir in the fresh coriander. Tip into a bowl and top with the crispy spiced onions. Very good with any kind of Indian bread or even warm pitta bread.

• You could also add a handful of chopped fresh spinach leaves towards the end of the cooking time.

FRESH CORIANDER CHUTNEY

If you make nothing else to go with your curry, make this.

1/2 large pack or bunch of coriander (about 75g)
2-3 sprigs of mint
About 3 large heaped tbsp plain, unsweetened low-fat yoghurt
1 clove of garlic, peeled and crushed with a little salt
1 chilli, de-seeded and finely chopped (*see* p35)
1-2 tsp fresh lemon juice
A pinch of ground cumin
Salt to taste

Wash the coriander thoroughly, shake dry then chop off the thicker stalks. Chop the leaves as finely as possible. Wash the mint, strip the leaves from the stalks and chop very finely too. Put the yoghurt in a bowl and mix in the mint, coriander, crushed garlic and chilli. Season to taste with salt, lemon juice and a little cumin if using. Cover and leave in the fridge for half an hour to let the flavours infuse. Eat within 2 hours of making it (which shouldn't be difficult).

- If you have a food processor or blender you can simply bung this all in together but don't overprocess it or you'll get something that resembles a pale green soup rather than a relish. Alternatively you can give it a bit of a whizz with a hand-held blender.

ONION AND CUCUMBER RAITA Serves 4-6

Most Indian restaurants offer either onion or cucumber raita. I like both but feel free to leave out the cucumber.

1 small onion, peeled and very finely sliced
1/4 cucumber, seeded and finely diced (*see* p31)
300ml low-fat yoghurt
1/4 tsp ground cumin
A pinch of chilli powder or cayenne pepper
1 tbsp lemon juice
Salt and extra cayenne pepper

Combine the onion, cucumber and yoghurt in a bowl. Mix well. Season with cumin, chilli powder or cayenne pepper, lemon juice and salt. Cover and set aside for 30 minutes for the flavours to infuse. Stir again and sprinkle lightly with chilli powder or cayenne pepper before serving.

Apart from kulfi (a delicious ice-cream with nuts), desserts aren't a major feature of most Indian restaurants which is a shame. But you can remedy that with the meals you make at home.

CARDAMOM RICE PUDDING WITH SHAVED MANGO 🌿

Serves 6-8

This tastes so good nobody will guess you opened a can. You can buy all the ingredients from an Asian grocer. Your mango should be ripe but not squishy otherwise you won't be able to cut it into strips.

2 x 425g cans luxury creamed rice pudding
1/2 level tsp of ground cardamom
1/2 tsp rosewater (optional)
2-3 tsp caster sugar
3 tbsp milk
1 large ripe (but not too ripe) mango

Open the cans of rice pudding and tip into a bowl with the milk and sugar. Stir then add the cardamom and a splash of rosewater if using. Check the seasoning adding extra cardamom, rosewater or sugar to taste. Peel the mango and take off long thin strips of the flesh with a vegetable peeler or, if the mango is very soft a sharp knife. Spoon the rice pudding into individual bowls and drape the mango slices artistically over the top.

FRESH TROPICAL FRUIT WITH MANGO SORBET 🌿 Serves 6-8

This couldn't be easier. All you need is ripe fruit.

A selection of the following depending on what's available or what you can afford: a small to medium ripe pineapple, a ripe mango, 1/2 a melon, a papaya, 2-3 star fruit, 4-6 passion fruit and 250g fresh lychees
2 x 500ml tubs of mango sorbet

Prepare and cut up all the fruit in advance (see below). Arrange on individual plates with a scoop of mango sorbet.

• Tinned tropical fruits like guavas and lychees can also be good though try to find ones that are canned with natural juice rather than syrup. (If you can't, drain the syrup and replace it with cardamom syrup or splash over a few drops of rosewater which you can buy in Asian shops).

How to choose and prepare exotic fruits

Pineapple
Choose pineapples that are orangey-brown rather than green. The flesh should 'give' slightly when you squeeze it. Cut a slice off the bottom and the leaves at the top, Holding the pineapple upright cut the coarse skin away. You'll still be left with some small bits of brown skin which you need to scoop out with the tip of a potato peeler or a sharp knife. Cut the pineapple in quarters and cut away the woody core down the centre then cut into slices or chunks.

Mango
Hold the mango upright and cut vertically down each side as near as you can get to the stone. Peel the slices you've made then cut away the rest of the flesh from around the stone. Cut into chunks without losing the juice, which is delicious.

Melon
Try to buy the more exotic varieties such as Canteloupe or Charentais rather than yellow-skinned honeydew. They should be scented when you sniff them. Quarter the fruit and scoop out the seeds. Cut the skin off if you want to serve them in chunks.

Papaya (paw paw)
The skin of ripe fruit should be yellow. Quarter the fruit and peel away the skin. The seeds are edible but you can remove them if you want.

Star fruit
Should be pale green, just beginning to go brown at the edges. Wash them, pat them dry then slice them thinly.

Passionfruit
Should have a dark, purplish wrinkly skin. (If they're not wrinkled they're unripe.) Cut in half. You can also spoon out the pulp for a sauce.

Lychees
Should be a dusky pink. Simply peel off the skin. They have a large stone in the middle so watch it when you're biting into them.

MANGO LASSI ♥
Serves 2-3

More like a smoothie than a dessert but just sensationally good. You do need a blender though.

1 large (500-550g) ripe mango
300ml very low-fat yoghurt
Juice of 1 lime (2 tbsp)
Chilled still mineral water

Peel the mango as described above. Place it in a blender or liquidiser together with 2 tablespoons of the yoghurt and whizz until smooth. Add the lime juice and remaining yoghurt and whizz again. Pour into a jug and gradually dilute to a drinkable consistency with the chilled mineral water (about 125ml). Stir and serve.

VEGETABLE SAMOSA PIE 🍁 Serves 6-8

This may look long and complicated but once you've got the hang of rolling out the pastry it's really not difficult, and it looks dead impressive. Feel free to vary the veg – potatoes and peas are a starting point but after that it's up to you. But don't skimp on the curry powder – if you can't find a good mix like the East End one I've mentioned (available in Safeway) use individual spices (see below).

750g new potatoes, scrubbed and halved or quartered into even sized pieces
3 tbsp sunflower or olive oil
1 medium-large onion (about 200-250g), peeled and finely chopped
2 tsp East End balti masala mix or other good quality curry spice blend
2 garlic cloves, peeled, crushed and finely chopped
150g frozen peas
4-5 heaped tbsp fresh coriander, chopped
Salt
2 medium eggs, lightly beaten
500g frozen puff pastry, thawed
A bit of plain flour

You will need a rectangular baking tray (about 27 x 37 cm). Boil the potatoes in boiling water for 10 minutes. Drain and cool. Heat the oil in a wok or large frying pan and fry the onion for about 7-8 minutes over a moderate heat until beginning to brown. Stir in the masala mix, cook for another few seconds then add the chopped garlic, peas and 3 tablespoons of water and leave to simmer for 5 minutes. Cut the cooked potatoes into small cubes then add to the pan. Heat through for a couple of minutes then crush them roughly with a fork. Stir in the chopped coriander and season with salt. Take the pan off the heat for a few minutes, mix in two thirds of the beaten egg then set aside to cool. Cut the pastry in two, making one half slightly bigger than the other. Sprinkle some flour on your (presumably clean) work surface and roll out the smaller half thinly. (Just keep rolling the pastry in different directions until you get a large even-sized rectangle.)

Trim the edges straight with a knife and lay on a lightly greased baking tray. Heat the oven to 220°C/425°F/Gas 7. Spoon the filling onto the pastry leaving a small border round the edges. Roll out the other half of the pastry so it is slightly bigger than the base. Brush or smear the exposed edges of the base with a little beaten egg, then carefully lower the top piece of pastry over the filling without stretching it and press the edges together. Trim off the overlapping pastry with a knife, then turning your knife round to the blunt side, drag the edges in at regular intervals round the edge of the pie to hold them together. Cut three vertical slits in the top of the pie and brush with the remaining beaten egg. Place the pie in the oven and cook for 15 minutes then lower the heat to 200°C/400°F/Gas 6 and cook for another 15-20 minutes until the pastry is well risen and brown. Serve hot or lukewarm with fresh coriander chutney and a salad.

- You can make the pie ahead and put it in the fridge but allow about 10 minutes extra cooking time.
- You could replace 250g of the potatoes with the same amount of lightly cooked carrots or a medium aubergine, cubed and fried in hot oil (about 3 tablespoons) for 5-6 minutes.
- If you have individual spices rather than a blend use a rounded teaspoon each of cumin and coriander, 1/2 tsp turmeric and 1/4 tsp chilli powder.

❁You can easily make the pie vegan by leaving out the egg.

The way to a man's heart, runs the old cliché, is through his stomach but the truth is it applies equally well to women. There's nothing so seductive – well almost nothing – as a guy who can cook. The following recipes should help to set the right tone for the evening: steak for those who feel a meal's not a meal without meat, and a wonderful mushroom dish for those who differ. Go for quality rather than quantity (I'm talking about the food here). Overdoing it on the food and drink front is more likely to send you to sleep than result in a night of torrid passion. And don't give yourself too much to do in the kitchen... for obvious reasons.

PEPPERED STEAK WITH RED WINE SAUCE Serves 2

If you're going to cook steak make it a good one. It's still cheaper than going out for a meal. Fillet is the easiest to cook but a decent rump steak would be fine.

½ tsp black peppercorns
2 thickly cut fillet steaks (about 200-250g each), trimmed of any excess fat
1 tbsp olive oil
75ml medium to full bodied red wine like a Chilean merlot
¼ tsp balsamic vinegar or a pinch of sugar
About 1 tsp soft butter
Sea salt

Crush the peppercorns coarsely and press them into either side of the steaks. Heat a frying pan for about 4 minutes until really hot. Add the oil to the pan, tilt it so it runs over the base, then add the steaks, pressing them down well. Cook for 2-3 minutes on either side depending whether you like them rare (5-6 minutes total) or medium to well done (8-9 minutes total). Remove the steaks from the pan and put them on warm plates to rest for a couple of minutes. Pour the wine into the pan and let it bubble up and reduce until it becomes thick and syrupy. Add the balsamic vinegar or sugar and butter. Pour in any juices that have run off the steak and check the seasoning, adding salt to taste and more pepper if you think it needs it. Pour the sauce over the steaks.

- This goes well with a mixed leaf salad with either the French or Italian dressings (see p56) and some garlic mash (see p110). You'll need to cook the mash before you start the steak (or buy ready-cooked mash from the supermarket). It's also very good with the Creamy Garlic Potato Bake (see p135) if you halve the quantities.
- If you don't want your steak quite as peppery as this just season it in the normal way with salt and freshly ground black pepper.
- Any wine you use for cooking should be drinkable. Take half a glass out of the bottle you buy to drink with the dish.

PORTABELLA MUSHROOM 'STEAKS' WITH GARLIC AND PARSLEY BUTTER ⓥ
Serves 2

Not literally steaks, obviously, but a more than satisfying meaty alternative for any vegetarian.

4 large, flat Portabella
   mushrooms (about 400g
   in total)
1/3 of a pack (about 85g)
   soft butter
2 garlic cloves
3 heaped tbsp finely chopped
   parsley
2 tbsp olive oil
Salt and pepper

Set the oven to 200°C/400°F/ Gas 6. Wipe the mushrooms and cut off the stalks with a sharp knife. Mash the butter in a bowl with the crushed garlic and finely chopped parsley, and season with salt and pepper. Pour 1 tablespoon of the olive oil into a baking dish large enough to take the mushrooms in a single layer. Lay out the mushrooms upside down. Divide the garlic butter between the mushrooms, spreading it evenly inside the cups. Drizzle the remaining olive oil over the edges of the mushrooms then bake for about 30 minutes until they are cooked through.

- This goes well with one of those ready-prepared potato bakes with rosemary which can cook at the same time. Or chips and a mixed leaf salad.

TRUFFLED MUSHROOM RISOTTO 🍂 Serves 2

Like learning to swim or ride a bicycle, risottos are one of those things that seem difficult but once you've got the hang of them are dead easy. And really, really impressive. The truffle oil might seem extravagant (it costs about £3-£3.50 a small bottle) but like perfume a little goes a very long way. (You can also use it in mashed potato or with mushroom pasta.)

1 small pack (about 25g) dried porcini mushrooms
125-150g open cap or chestnut mushrooms
1 small onion or ½ medium onion, peeled and finely chopped
1 clove of garlic (optional)
40g butter
150g Arborio, Carnaroli or Vialone Nano (i.e. authentic Italian) risotto rice
½ glass (about 75ml) dry white wine
500ml vegetable stock or stock made with 2 level tsp Marigold vegetable bouillon powder
Salt and pepper
1 tbsp fromage frais, Quark or whipping or double cream
2 tbsp fresh parsley, chopped (optional)
White or black truffle oil

Before you start the recipe soak the porcini in about 175ml warm water for 20 minutes to half an hour. Rinse the mushrooms, trim the stalks and chop roughly. Peel and finely chop the onion. Peel and crush the garlic if using. Drain the dried mushrooms through a tea strainer reserving the soaking water, and chop them roughly too. Melt the butter over a medium heat in a large saucepan, add the chopped onion and cook gently until soft (about 5 minutes). Add the fresh mushrooms and garlic if using, stir well, turn the heat up a little and cook for a couple of minutes. Add the dried mushrooms and cook for another minute or two.

Tip in the rice, stir and cook for 2-3 minutes until the grains have turned opaque and are beginning to catch on the bottom of the pan. Add the wine, stir and let it bubble up and evaporate. Meanwhile heat the reserved mushroom water until boiling then add half of that, continuing to stir. Once the liquid has evaporated add the remaining mushroom stock then bring the vegetable stock to the boil and keep at a simmer. Keep adding cupfuls of stock every time the liquid in the risotto gets absorbed. Stir until it starts to look creamy and the rice tastes neither hard and chalky nor soggy. (This should take about 20 minutes. You might not need all the stock.) Turn the heat off then check the seasoning, adding salt and pepper and a spoonful or two of fromage frais, Quark or cream. Cover the pan and let the flavours amalgamate for 2-3 minutes then spoon the risotto into warm bowls. Sprinkle with a little finely chopped parsley and trickle over a tiny bit of truffle oil.

- The secret of a good risotto is 'toasting' the rice (i.e. cooking it with the butter, onions and mushrooms) before you add any liquid, making sure the liquid you add is at boiling point and stirring continuously but not too frantically.
- I don't think this needs Parmesan but you can add it if you want.

SALMON WITH ROASTED PEPPERS AND GARLIC Serves 2

A really simple main course that looks fabulously cheffy. You have to both like garlic, though.

2 small to medium red peppers
2-3 tbsp extra virgin olive oil
3 cloves of garlic, peeled and thinly sliced
Salt and pepper
2 boneless salmon fillets (about 350g)
A few fresh basil leaves
1/2 pack of spinach and watercress salad or rocket salad

Preheat oven to 180°C/350°F/Gas 4. Cut each pepper in quarters, removing the stalk and white flesh. Pour 1 tablespoon of the oil over the base of a large roasting tin and lay the peppers in a single layer, cut sides upwards. Place a couple of slices of garlic on each piece of pepper, season with salt and pepper and trickle over the remaining oil. Bake for 30-40 minutes until the peppers are beginning to look charred. Remove the dish from the oven and push the peppers to the sides of the dish. Dip both sides of each salmon fillet in the warm garlicky oil then lay them in the tin, skin side downwards. Season with salt and pepper, tuck about half the basil leaves under the fish and roast for a further 15 minutes. Arrange the salmon and peppers on two plates with a handful of salad leaves. Stir the pan juices and trickle them over the leaves. Decorate the fish with the remainder of the basil leaves, roughly torn. Serve with new potatoes or crusty bread.

Never mind how old you are there's an eternal appeal in ice-cream and jelly. Not served lukewarm on a paper plate the way you had it when you were five, obviously. Dress it up with a shot of vodka, a luscious fruit sauce or a few slices of fresh fruit and serve it in a frosted cocktail or wine glass and you've got yourself an unbelievably classy dessert.

ICED VODKA AND LEMON SORBET ♥
Serves 2

This looks fantastic in frozen martini glasses. Pick up a couple of cheap ones and leave them in the freezer compartment until you're ready to serve up (or if there isn't room fill them with ice and a little water then chuck it out and dry them).

2-3 tbsp frozen vodka (keep in the freezer compartment until you need it)
A carton of good quality lemon sorbet

Take the sorbet out of the freezer and put it in the fridge about 20 minutes before you plan to serve it. (This makes it soft enough to scoop). Spoon out a couple of generous scoops and place them in the frosted glass. Pour over the frozen vodka. Await gasps of admiration.

• You can obviously make this with other sorbets. Raspberry goes well with vodka too.

ICED PAVLOVAS WITH FRESH ORANGE AND PASSION FRUIT SAUCE
Ⓥ Serves 2

2 passion fruit
1 tbsp freshly squeezed orange juice
1 tsp caster sugar
2 meringue nests (Marks and Sparks have particularly good ones)
4 scoops of top quality vanilla ice cream
A few drops of orange flower water (optional)

Halve the passion fruit and scoop the pulp and seeds into a small bowl, taking care not to remove any of the bitter pith. Add the orange juice and sugar and stir. Check for sweetness adding a few drops of orange flower water and/or extra sugar to taste. Put a meringue nest on each plate, top with the vanilla ice-cream and spoon over the orange and passion fruit sauce.

SPARKLING RASPBERRY JELLY

Serves 2

Even basic jellies can be made to taste sensational if you add a little sparkling wine to them. This couldn't be easier – all you need to remember is to add the fruit at the moment it's about to set so it doesn't drop down to the bottom.

1/2 135g pack of raspberry jelly
75g frozen raspberries
1 tsp fresh lemon juice
1 chilled bottle of Cava or other inexpensive sparkling wine

Cut the jelly into cubes (easiest with kitchen scissors) and place in a measuring jug. Add 2 tablespoons of water and heat or microwave on high for 1 1/2 minutes until the jelly has melted. Open the Cava and pour into the jug, up to the 275ml mark. Add the lemon juice and stir. Leave to cool for about 1/2 an hour then put it into the fridge for another hour or so until just beginning to set. (It should wobble slightly when you shake it). Take the raspberries out of the freezer and let them thaw very slightly till you can separate them. Stir them into the jelly then spoon it into individual glasses or glass dishes. Return to the fridge until set. Serve on their own or with a jug of cream.

• If you don't use the rest of the Cava immediately (unlikely, I admit) drink it with the Smoked Salmon Pizza (see p168).

SPARKLING PEACH, NECTARINE AND BLUEBERRY JELLY

Serves 2

Don't be daunted – gelatine is really easy to use and you'll get a much more natural flavour.

2 sheets of gelatine
275ml low-alcohol sparkling peach wine cocktail
1/2 ripe nectarine
1 tsp lemon juice
50g fresh blueberries

Place the gelatine in a flat dish and pour over 2 tablespoons of cold water. Heat the peach cocktail in a microwave or saucepan until hot but not boiling. Tip the gelatine into the peach wine and stir to dissolve. Place in the fridge, as above, to set. When just about at setting point, cut round the nectarine and twist each half in opposite directions to pull them apart. Cut one half into cubes and pour the lemon juice over it. Rinse the blueberries and stir them and the nectarine into the jelly. Spoon into glasses as above.

Some things are just not worth making from scratch. There are so many great chocolate desserts and cakes out there that it would be crazy to slave away whipping up a chocolate mousse or a chocolate tart just for two. But what's really worth making are recipes where it's crucial for the choccy to be hot – or at least warm.

WICKED CHOCOLATE SAUCE 🍁 Serves 2

The perfect dark chocolate sauce to pour over ice-cream... or your partner (having let it cool down first, of course).

100g dark luxury Belgian
  chocolate
75 ml whipping cream
1 level tbsp icing sugar

Break the chocolate into squares and put it in a bowl with the cream. Fit the bowl over a saucepan that has a little boiling water in the bottom (the base of the bowl shouldn't touch the water). Place the saucepan over a low to moderate heat. Stir the chocolate and cream until the chocolate melts. Sift in the icing sugar (use a tea strainer) and add 1-2 tablespoons of water to give you a pouring consistency.

• The best and least expensive place to find good chocolate is the baking section of the supermarket. Luxury Belgian chocolate is particularly good.

FROSTED BERRIES WITH WHITE CHOCOLATE AND CARDAMOM SAUCE
🍁 Serves 2

This brilliant idea came from Mark Hix, the chef at London's famous Ivy restaurant. I've added the cardamom which I think makes it even better.

75g white Belgian chocolate
  (see above)
1/2 small carton of double cream
  (about 5 tbsp)
1/4 tsp ground cardamom
  (available from Asian grocers)
  or 2 cardamom pods, husks
  removed and seeds finely
  crushed
150g frozen raspberries or 75g
  frozen raspberries and 75g
  fresh blueberries
1/2 tsp cocoa powder (optional)

Put the chocolate in a bowl with the cream and fit it over a saucepan with a little boiling water in the bottom (*see opposite*). Place the saucepan over a low to moderate heat. Stir the chocolate and cream until the chocolate melts then stir in the cardamom. Divide the raspberries between two plates and leave for 5 minutes to begin to thaw. Pour over the warm chocolate sauce. Sieve the cocoa powder, if using, over the top with a tea strainer.

WARM CHOCOLATE CHIP COOKIES ✿

Makes about 30-35 cookies

Nothing compares to home made cookies, straight from the oven so the chocolate is all warm and gooey. This makes far more than two people can possibly eat but if you're taking the trouble to bake you might as well make a big batch.

125g dark luxury Belgian chocolate
125g soft butter (at room temperature)
75g soft light brown sugar
50g granulated sugar
1 large egg
1/2 tsp vanilla extract (optional)
165g plain flour
1/2 tsp bicarbonate of soda
1/4 tsp salt

Preheat the oven to 180°C/350°F/Gas 4. You'll need at least one, preferably two baking trays. Break the chocolate into chunks then cut it into smaller chips with a knife. Beat the butter and sugars together in a large bowl until light and fluffy. Lightly beat the egg in another bowl or mug, add the vanilla if using then add it to the butter mixture bit by bit, beating all the time. Mix in the flour, salt and bicarbonate of soda then add the chopped chocolate. Drop 8-9 teaspoons of the mixture on a baking tray leaving plenty of space in between each spoonful.

Bake for 10-12 minutes until browned. Remove the tray from the oven, leave for a couple of minutes then prise off the cookies with a knife and transfer them to a wire rack. (Use an oven shelf or the rack on a grill pan if you don't have one). Repeat with the next batch of cookies. Serve warm on their own or with vanilla ice-cream.

! If you bake two trays at the same time the lower tray may cook more slowly than the top one, especially in a gas oven, so it will need extra time.

• You can make white chocolate chip cookies by replacing the dark chocolate with white chocolate and adding a tablespoon of sifted cocoa to the flour.

Your ability to rustle up something delicious the morning after should consolidate the gains of the night before. Top of the list for most men will be a full-blown fry-up, particularly if you can make it as well as, if not better than, his mum.

THE ULTIMATE FRY-UP

Like a roast, a fry-up isn't difficult, merely a question of organisation and having the right ingredients. Which are: A big frying pan – the biggest possible, preferably non-stick. A light cooking oil (sunflower or rapeseed) and a little butter for the eggs. Plus...

Sausages

Buy thin chipolatas – they'll cook quicker. Turn them regularly so they don't burn, and don't prick them. (5-6 minutes.)

Bacon

If you're pulling out the stops buy dry-cure bacon which won't go wet and soggy in the pan. (Personally I like streaky but it's up to you.) If you've only got basic bacon, microwave it first to get rid of the gunk. To do this, lay the rashers in a single layer on a plate, cover loosely with a sheet of kitchen towel and cook for about 2 minutes on a moderate setting. Fish out the rashers, pat dry with kitchen towel and grill or fry on both sides until crisp.

(3-4 minutes once you've microwaved them.)

Eggs

Should be at least free range and definitely fresh. Cook last (see p52). (3-4 minutes.)

Mushrooms

Buy the open flat type. Wipe clean and either grill or fry in a mixture of oil and butter. Cook after (or instead of) the sausages. (4-5 minutes.)

Tomatoes

Include only if ripe. Cut them in half, place cut side down and fry for 3-4 minutes. Turn and season with salt and pepper. Cook for another 2-3 minutes.

Fried bread

(If you must. Toast is nicer and less fatty.) Make sure you have at least a centimetre of oil in the pan. Heat it until very hot then drop in two slices of bread. Fry about a minute then turn them over and fry the other side. Remove and drain on kitchen paper. Discard the excess oil.

Black pudding

Buy ready-sliced and fry or grill for about 2-3 minutes a side.

Cook in the following order: Fried bread, sausages, black pudding and mushrooms, bacon and tomatoes (if you can grill them this takes a bit of pressure off) then finally the eggs. Keep the bits of the fry-up you've cooked on a warm plate under a piece of foil.

AMERICAN BREAKFAST PANCAKES WITH BLUEBERRIES 🍁
Serves 2-4

A slightly less macho offering. Don't be daunted if you've never made pancakes before. These are a doddle.

125g plain flour
2 level tsp caster sugar
$1/4$ level tsp fine sea salt
$1^1/2$ level tsp baking powder
1 large fresh free range egg
150ml whole (i.e. not skimmed or semi-skimmed) milk
40g of butter, melted
1 x 125g carton blueberries
A small carton of Greek yoghurt or plain low-fat fromage frais
Some clear honey

To make the pancakes mix the first 4 ingredients together in a bowl leaving a hollow in the centre. Lightly beat the egg, mix with the milk and a tablespoon of the melted butter and gradually pour into the flour stirring with a wooden spoon until it is mixed in. Don't worry if it looks a bit lumpy.

Heat a non-stick frying pan over a moderate heat, pour in a little of the remaining melted butter and spread it over the pan with a piece of kitchen towel. Place four tablespoons of the pancake mixture into the pan, leaving a space between them. Let them cook for about a minute until bubbles begin to appear on the surface, then flip them over with a spatula and cook them for 45 seconds on the other side. Stack them on a plate covered with a clean tea-towel and repeat the process until all the mixture is used up, greasing the pan with melted butter before you cook each batch. Place three or four pancakes on each plate, with a mound of blueberries and a dollop of fromage frais or yoghurt, drizzled with a little honey.

- If you're really into pancakes and fancy mastering everything from tossing to toppings, then read on to pp170-171.

If you don't emerge till midday – or even mid afternoon – here's something more akin to a lunch.

SMOKED SALMON PIZZA WITH CREAM CHEESE AND ROCKET

Serves 2

The best recipes look impressive but are in fact ridiculously easy. This is one of them. You may think one pizza is a bit stingy for two but the cream cheese makes it quite rich. (Double the recipe if you're not convinced).

1½ tbsp extra virgin olive oil
1 ready to cook thin and crispy
    pizza base (available from
    the pizza section)
125g cream cheese
1½ tbsp milk
2 tsp very finely chopped onion
    (optional but good)
Freshly ground black pepper
A small (150g) pack of wafer
    thin smoked salmon
    (or ordinary sliced smoked
    salmon, see below)
A quarter of a lemon or about
    2 tsp lemon juice
A small pack of rocket

Using a little of the oil, brush the pizza base lightly on each side. Cook for one minute each side under a moderate grill. Set aside on a rack and cool for 15 minutes. Turn the cream cheese into a bowl and mash up with the milk so you get a soft, spreading consistency. Add the chopped onion, if using, and season with freshly ground black pepper (you shouldn't need salt as smoked salmon is quite salty). When the base has cooled down spread it with the cream cheese mixture then drape the smoked salmon pieces artistically over the top. Squeeze a little lemon juice over the salmon and season with black pepper. Take a handful of rocket leaves and pile them on top of the smoked salmon. Trickle a little olive oil over the leaves.

- It can be worth buying a large pack of smoked salmon. At certain times of year (e.g. Valentine's Day) it's not much more expensive than a small pack. You can use the leftovers in scrambled eggs, with pasta (see p44) or in an Mozzarella, Avocado and Tomato Salad (see p58).

GRILLED CIABATTA WITH MOZZARELLA, CHERRY TOMATOES AND PESTO DRIZZLE

Serves 2

Poshed up cheese and tomatoes on toast, basically.

125g cherry tomatoes
125g ball of authentic Italian Mozzarella
1 tbsp extra virgin olive oil
Salt and freshly ground black pepper
4-6 basil leaves
A few rocket or watercress leaves
1/2 ciabatta

For the pesto drizzle
2 tsp green pesto
2 tsp fresh lemon juice
3 tbsp olive oil

Halve the cherry tomatoes, cut the Mozzarella into chunks and marinate in a bowl with 1 tablespoon of olive oil and some salt and pepper, for 15-20 minutes to allow the flavours to develop. Whisk the pesto sauce with 2 teaspoons of water and the lemon juice then whisk in the olive oil. Cut the halved ciabatta in half lengthways. Lightly grill the two halves crust side up then turn over and spread the other sides with half the pesto dressing. Replace under the grill and toast lightly for a minute. Place each piece of ciabatta on a plate and pile on the other ingredients starting with a handful of rocket, then the tomato and Mozzarella mixture then a couple of leaves of torn basil. Grind over a little extra black pepper then spoon over the remaining pesto drizzle.

Just as cooking a Sunday lunch gives you a warm fuzzy feeling, so does celebrating other food-related milestones of the year like pancake day and bonfire night. It actually makes sense financially too. Supermarkets always put on promotions round about these times to get us through their doors so the ingredients you need are likely to be cheap.

(Not all celebrations fall within the university term of course so I've left out Easter but if you want to hold your own pre-Christmas celebration *see* p132.)

Pancake Day

Shrove Tuesday is one of those dates that's a moveable feast depending when Easter falls but it's usually somewhere around the middle to end of February.

CRUNCHY LEMON PANCAKES

Makes 6-8 large pancakes

The classic pancake day pancake. 'Crunchy' should remind you to use granulated rather than caster sugar. Tastes much better.

110g plain flour
1/4 tsp salt
2 large fresh free-range eggs
275ml semi-skimmed milk
25g cooled melted butter plus another 25g melted butter for greasing the pan

For serving

2 lemons cut into quarters
Granulated sugar

Mix the flour and salt in a large bowl. Make a hollow in the centre. Beat the eggs lightly with the milk then add 25g cool melted butter. Gradually pour the mixture into the flour, stirring all the time, and beat well with a wooden spoon. Set the batter aside for 1/2 an hour then beat again. Heat the pan until quite hot, then grease it with some scrunched-up kitchen towel dipped in the remaining butter. Add a small chunk of butter and rub it round the pan with some scrunched-up kitchen towel. Scoop out a small cup or 1/3 of a mug of batter and tip it into the pan swirling it round quickly so the whole base of the pan is covered with batter. Cook for about 30 seconds till the edges begin to brown then flip over with a spatula and cook the other side. Serve up straight away as you make them, squeezing on lemon and sprinkling with about a teaspoon of granulated sugar, then rolling them up or folding them into four.

Other indulgent things you can put on a pancake

- Golden syrup.
- Wicked Chocolate Sauce (see p164).
- Bananas cooked with butter and soft brown sugar (see p76).
- Warm apple and cinnamon compote (see p77) and cream.
- Soft set cherry jam and vanilla ice-cream.

The right kit

It's easiest to make pancakes in a special low-sided pancake pan which makes them easier to turn. If you're into pancakes it may be worth buying one at this time of year when they're likely to be on promotion. Otherwise use a large clean non-stick frying pan that hasn't got bits of burnt on sausage adhering to it otherwise your pancakes will break up.

The right temperature

The crucial thing with pancakes is getting the temperature right. The pan needs to be quite hot so the batter runs freely over it when you pour it in. To help with this, add a small chunk of butter and rub it round the pan with some scrunched-up kitchen towel between each pancake. The first pancake you make with probably be a dud but after that you should be able to turn out ones that look impressively professional.

How to toss a pancake

Ease a spatula round the sides of the pancake to make sure it's not stuck to the bottom. Give the pan a good shake then hold the handle with both hands and jerk it upwards towards you so the pancake flips over. Be prepared to move the pan to catch it in mid-flight and don't try to toss it too high!

Hallowe'en and Bonfire Night
Since these occur within days of each other (October 31st and November 5th) you can celebrate the two together. Bangers and mash are always a winner, but if you want to be a bit more adventurous try one of these substantial spicy soups.

HOT CHILLI BUTTERNUT SQUASH SOUP 🍁 Serves 4

Butternut squash tastes a lot nicer than pumpkin and makes a fabulous brilliant orange velvety soup.

1 butternut squash
   (about 750-850g)
3 tbsp sunflower or light olive oil
1 medium to large onion roughly
   chopped
1 clove of garlic, crushed
1 tbsp Moroccan Spice Mix
   (see p35)
1 400g can chopped tomatoes
600ml (1 pint) stock made
   with 2 tsp Marigold vegetable
   bouillon powder or a stock
   cube
1/2-1 tsp hot pepper sauce
Salt

To serve
1 small carton sour cream
2-3 tbsp coriander leaves,
   roughly chopped

Heat the oven to 190°C/375°F/ Gas 5. Rinse the butternut squash under the cold tap, dry it then cut it in half lengthways with a large knife and scoop out the seeds. Put 1 tablespoon of the oil in a roasting tin then lay the two halves in the tin cut side down. Bake for about 40 minutes until soft. Remove from the oven and set aside for 10-15 minutes until cool enough to handle. Meanwhile fry the onion gently for 10 minutes in the other two tablespoons of oil until soft. Add the crushed garlic and Moroccan Spice Mix, cook for a minute then tip in the chopped tomatoes and cook for about 5 minutes until thick and jammy. Scoop the pulp out of the squash. Place half of it in a blender or food processor along with half the spiced tomato mixture, a bit of stock and any juices in the baking tin and whizz until smooth. Repeat with the remaining ingredients (you may even have to do this in three batches). Pour the soup back into a large saucepan and stir in the rest of the stock. Add hot sauce and salt to taste. To serve, pour the soup into bowls, spoon over a swirl of sour cream and scatter over a few coriander leaves.

- If you have a hand-held blender cook the onion/tomato mixture in a large saucepan, add the cooked squash to it then blitz it in the pan.

THREE-CAN CHILLI BEAN SOUP 🍁 Serves 4-6

This is a bit like a chilli con carne without the meat. Don't be daunted by the list of ingredients. You don't need all the toppings.

2 large onions (about 350g)
3 tbsp light olive or sunflower oil
2 large cloves of garlic
1 tbsp mild chilli powder
1 tsp ground cumin
1 400g can chopped tomatoes
1 400g can borlotti beans, drained and rinsed
1 400g can red kidney beans, drained and rinsed
750ml vegetable stock made with 1 tbsp Marigold vegetable bouillon powder or a stock cube
Salt and hot pepper sauce

To serve, any or all of the following

A 200g packet of tortilla chips, some broken up for sprinkling, others whole for dunking
Chopped coriander leaves
Some crumbled mild white cheese like Cheshire or Wensleydale and/or some grated Cheddar
1 finely chopped red onion
Sour cream
Wedges of lemon or lime
More hot pepper sauce

Peel and roughly chop the onions. Heat the oil in a large deep saucepan or casserole and fry the onions over a medium heat for about ten minutes until moderately brown. Add the crushed garlic, chilli powder and cumin, stir and cook for another minute. Add the chopped tomatoes, drained and rinsed beans and 250ml of the stock, bring to the boil and simmer for 10 minutes. Cool slightly then whizz in a blender or food processor, adding a little more stock if necessary to make a smooth purée (you may have to do this in two or three batches). Return to the pan adding the remainder of the stock and reheat. Check the seasoning adding salt and hot pepper sauce to taste. Prepare as many of the toppings as you like and put them in individual bowls. Serve up the soup and let everyone add the toppings they want.

- If you don't want to make such a performance of it just serve the soup with a swirl of sour cream, chopped coriander and some crumbled tortilla chips.

Other dates to celebrate:

Burns Night (January 25th) Attempt a haggis (you can get vegetarian ones) and Bashed Neeps (see p111).

Chinese New Year (early February) Buy in some Chinese-style snacks like prawn toasts and spring rolls and double or treble the quantities of the Extremely Easy Stir-Fry (see p51).

St Patrick's Day (March 17th) Cumberland Sausages with Rich Guinness Gravy (see p96).

BEYOND BAD BOOZE

Quantity rather than quality being the time-honoured name of the game for student drinking it might seem a bit odd to have a section on drink. But just as you can eat better at home than in most restaurants you can afford, you can drink better too. And if you drink better you're likely to drink less which can't be a bad thing.

Here's the know-how you need to impress – the best student wines, beers and spirits and a few killer cocktails to make with them.

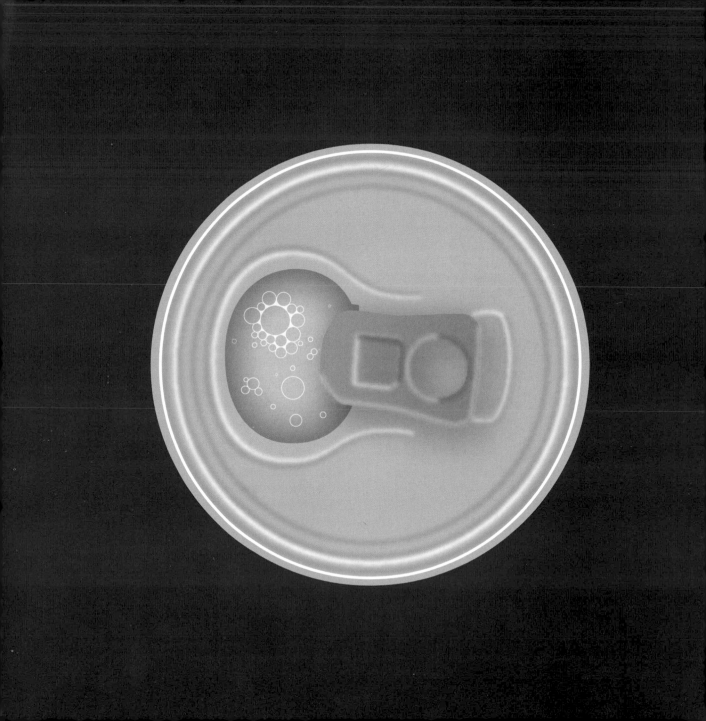

The same rules apply to buying wine as apply to food.

- Own brands are a good starting point – often better value than big brands unless they're on special offer.
- Unfashionable countries like Bulgaria and Romania are generally better value than popular ones like Chile and Australia.
- Because so much of the price of a bottle goes on fixed costs like bottling, tax and duty, the more you pay for a wine the more goes on the wine itself. So if you can run to it aim to spend £3-4 a bottle rather than under £3.

GOOD CHEAP WHITES

Good news all the way. Cheap whites have never been better. Even those labelled simply 'dry white' (as in Australian dry white or Chilean dry white) are more than drinkable. If you're a Chardonnay fan the best place to buy from is Eastern Europe, especially Bulgaria and Hungary whose wines are often made by Australian-trained winemakers. A good tip is to buy Chardonnay blended with another grape like Chenin Blanc or Colombard or something else unpronounceable you've never heard of. Keeps the cost down.

GOOD CHEAP REDS

There are plenty of options here too. France still delivers great drinking for under £4, especially from the Languedoc (look out for Fitou, Minervois and Corbières and wines labelled Vin de Pays d'Oc). If you like a soft fruity style of red go for the Merlot. Other excellent sources of feisty reds are Spain, southern Italy and Sicily, Bulgaria, Romania and Argentina. And own-brand Claret is surprisingly good value – it's a wine the supermarkets bend over backwards to get right.

GOOD CHEAP ROSÉ

Don't dismiss rosé as for wimps. These days many are as robust as a light red wine and make great drinking in the summer (when they're always on promotion). Like reds, the best areas to buy from are southern France, Spain and Eastern Europe.

GOOD CHEAP FIZZ

Cava, a dry sparkling wine from Spain, is the out-and-out winner here. Look for Champagne bargains in the run-up to Valentine's Day.

THE 10 BEST STUDENT WINE BUYS FOR UNDER £4

Hungarian Chardonnay
Lighter than Aussie chard' but great value.
Vin de pays des Côtes de Gascogne
An underrated fresh, fruity French white.
South African Chenin Blanc
A cut-price alternative to Chardonnay.
Sicilian White
Nice'n'easy. Smooth'n'dry.
Argentinian Torrontes
Exotic, perfumed and flowery.
Bulgarian Cabernet Sauvignon
The cut-price version of the world's most famous red wine grape.
Spanish Tempranillo
The grape that's used to make Rioja. Full and rich.
Californian Ruby Cabernet
Lush, sweet and jammy.
Romanian Pinot Noir
Rich, dark and spicy.
Moscatel de Valencia
Sweet and grapey. The best value dessert wine around.

WINE KIT

The only essential is a corkscrew – even though many wines are now being bottled in screwcap. The cheapest kind is the so-called 'waiter's friend', but it's not the easiest to use. What you ideally want is one that does the hard work of pulling the cork out of the bottle for you, which will cost more like a tenner. Add it to your wish list. In theory, wine glasses should have a big bowl that tapers towards the top and a long stem, but since they'll almost certainly get broken I'd go for a short chunky glass. If you like trawling charity shops for bargains, pick them up individually.
Glasses – and plates – are always cheaper if you don't buy a matching set.

HOW TO OPEN A BOTTLE OF BUBBLY

Make sure the bottle is well chilled before you start. Remove the foil and wire that hold the cork. Point the bottle away from you (and anyone else). Holding on to the cork with your left hand twist the base of the bottle with your right hand. (Or vice-versa if you're left-handed.) You should feel the cork begin to ease out. Continue to cup your hand over the cork and let the pressure in the bottle push the cork out. (You should get a quiet 'phut' rather than a bang.) Have a glass to hand in case the bubbles overflow. Tilt the glass towards your pouring hand and pour steadily.

! Don't jiggle the bottle up and down like a racing driver before you take the cork out – you'll lose half the contents.

HOW TO TELL IF A WINE IS 'CORKED'

A surprisingly large number of wines are 'corked'. That doesn't mean the wine has little bits of cork floating around in it but that it has been contaminated by a faulty cork. It won't do you any harm but it will smell slightly mouldy and taste pretty foul. Which is why you should always sniff a wine in a restaurant and ask them to replace it if it's faulty. *Before* you drink it.

A FEW THINGS TO SAY
ABOUT BEER AND CIDER

Given the choice between spending £1 per pint of bog-standard beer in the union bar or twice as much elsewhere on something more interesting you're probably not going to spend a lot of time agonising over the decision. But it's worth bearing the following in mind:

- Own brands are better value than big brands. The same old story – don't be seduced by the ads.
- Real ale is better than cans. That doesn't make you a beer anorak, merely a consumer of taste. (Is freshly squeezed orange juice better than a carton from your local supermarket's 'value' range? You bet it is.)
- IPA (Indian pale ale) goes better than lager with a curry.
- The Germans and Czechs make the best lager of all.
- If you don't think you like beer try a light citrussy wheat beer like Hoegaarden. Add equal amounts of traditonal lemonade for a really refreshing shandy.
- Sparkling cider from Normandy is a great substitute for sparkling wine. Even cheaper than Cava.
- Beer and cider have their place in the kitchen. *See* the recipe for A Good Old-Fashioned Pub Stew (p100) *and* don't miss the Cumberland Sausages with Guinness Gravy (p96).

COCKTAILS, SPIRITS AND OTHER STRONG DRINKS

Even if you don't cook it's fun making cocktails. (And if you can make good cocktails you can cook – so no excuse). That doesn't mean you should go mad and pour in everything but the kitchen sink. The best cocktail recipes are quite simple – relying on two or three well-balanced ingredients.

Ideally you should make cocktails individually, but that's not really practical when you're making them for more than two or three people. In which case, mix them in a large jug. As well as a jug then, you'll also need the following:

- Ice – and far more than you think. A good cocktail needs to be shaken with ice or at least poured into a jug full of ice. Buy a big bag (or two) for any cocktail session. If you haven't got enough room in your freezer you can keep it cold for a couple of hours in...
- ...a cool box (essential for parties – and picnics)
- A shaker (or a large jam jar) and a fine strainer (a tea strainer will do) to strain out bits of broken ice and fruit. If you use a jam jar you'll also need a measuring spoon. Two tablespoons = a shot. Otherwise, use the top of the shaker as a measure.
- A rolling pin – for making crushed ice (wrap it in a clean tea-towel then bash it) and for 'muddling' (i.e. crushing) mint leaves and fresh fruit.
- Martini glasses (if you want to show off).
- Sugar syrup. This will make your drink sweet without making it gritty. Measure 125g of unrefined (golden) granulated sugar and put into a pan with 125ml of water. Warm it over a very low heat, stirring occasionally until all the sugar crystals dissolve. Take the pan off the heat. Cool the syrup then pour into a clean jam jar and put it in the fridge. It should keep for a couple of weeks.
- Freshly squeezed lime and lemon juice. Certainly in any cocktail where they're a key ingredient. Just prior to using, roll them under the palm of your hand on a flat surface to maximise the amount of juice.
- Access to the internet. There are masses of cocktail sites with free recipes including **www.knowyourcocktails.com** and the US-based **www.cocktail.com**. I also recommend the *Sauce Guide to Cocktails* which has over 1,400 recipes including all the newest cocktails from London bars.

BARGAIN BOTTLES

A few tips that should help keep costs down.

- Own-brand spirits are a good £3-4 cheaper than the well-known brands. Check the strength though – most cocktail recipes are based on using spirits that are 40% ABV.
- Vermouth – so out of fashion it's ridiculously cheap. Secco is the type you use with a classic martini (just a whisper). Sweeter Bianco and Rosso can be mixed 50/50 with other ingredients for a long refreshing drink (try Bianco with soda and Rosso with cranberry juice).
- Ginger wine – great for winter drinking. Mix it with whisky for a warming Whisky Mac.
- Own-brand Irish cream liqueur. Much cheaper than Bailey's. Serve straight from the fridge.
- White port – quite scarce, but worth picking up if you can find it at a reasonable price. Dilute with tonic to taste (about 50/50) and serve it over ice the way the Portuguese do.
- Montilla – from the same part of Spain as sherry but even cheaper. The medium-dry is especially appealing.

COCKTAILS

Spirit + sugar + lime
= a universal formula

These three ingredients are at the heart of the world's most popular cocktails, notably the Margarita (tequila), Daiquiri and mojito (rum) and caiprinha (made with the Brazilian national spirit, cachaca). If you can make these well you can make anything.

The recipes on the following pages all serve one. Feel free to alter the amounts of lime juice and sugar to your own taste.

MARGARITA

The world's most popular cocktail.

50ml (3 tbsp) tequila
25ml (1½ tbsp) lime juice
25ml (1½ tbsp) Cointreau
  or triple sec
Coarse sea salt (optional)

Place the ingredients in a shaker or jam jar with 1 tablespoon of water. Fill the shaker with ice. Shake vigorously and strain into a glass. To make a frozen margarita blend the ingredients with crushed ice (you need a powerful blender for this). It's traditional to serve a margarita in a salted glass but don't feel bound to.

- To salt a glass run half a lime round the rim of the glass then press it into a plate of salt.
- You can also make fresh fruit margaritas – strawberry is particularly good.

DAIQUIRI
(PRONOUNCED DIE-KERREE)

A Cuban classic.

50ml (3 tbsp) light or dark rum
20ml (1¼ tbsp) freshly
  squeezed lime juice
1½-2 tsp sugar syrup
  (see p180)

Follow the method for the Margarita, above. You can make frozen Daiquiris the same way as a frozen margarita.

MOJITO
(PRONOUNCED MO-HEATOE)

Another Cuban favourite. Great summer drinking.

2 sprigs of fresh mint
1½-2 tsp sugar or sugar syrup
  (see p180)
25ml (1½ tbsp) lime juice
50ml (3 tbsp) rum
Soda water
Angostura bitters (optional)

Strip the leaves off the stalks of the mint sprigs. Place in the bottom of a chunky glass, add the sugar and 'muddle' or pound (gently) with a pestle or the base of a rolling pin to crush the mint leaves. Add the lime juice, 3 cubes of crushed ice and the rum and a few drops of Angostura bitters if you have some. Stir and top up with soda.

CAIPIRINHA
(PRONOUNCED KY-PIREENYA)

Brazil's national drink.

1 lime, preferably unwaxed
1½-2 tsp sugar syrup
  (see p180) or sugar
50ml cachaca or white rum

Wash the lime and cut into 8 pieces. Put in the bottom of a glass with the sugar syrup and pound to extract the oils from the skin (see Mojito, above). Add 3 crushed ice cubes, pour in the cachaca and stir.

- A caipirinha made with vodka is called a caipirosca.

And if I don't like lime?

Are you mad? Try these then. Each makes roughly a litre – enough for 4-6 glasses.

SEA BREEZE

Just about the best summer cocktail to have been invented in recent years.

300ml vodka
400ml cranberry juice
300ml grapefruit juice

Pour the ingredients into a large jug full of ice. Stir.

! Filling a jug – or glass – with ice is not as extravagant as it sounds. The colder your drinks stay, the less diluted it will get and the better it will taste.

RUM PUNCH

The classic formula for a Jamaican rum punch is one of sour (lemon or lime juice), two of sweet (sugar syrup or grenadine), three of strong (rum, of course) and four of weak (some kind of fruit juice or water). Personally I prefer a slightly less sweet drink so I make the sweet component the same as the sour but it's up to you.

100ml freshly squeezed
   lemon juice
100ml sugar syrup (*see* p180)
   or grenadine
300ml golden or dark rum
400ml tropical fruit juice

Follow method for Sea Breeze. Float some slices of orange, lemon or apple in if you want.

• Grenadine is a non-alcoholic (or occasionally low-alcohol) syrup made from pomegranates which gives a lovely deep colour to cocktails.

WHITE SANGRIA

A bit like a floating fruit salad but brilliantly refreshing.

1 bottle basic dry Spanish –
   or French – white wine, chilled
5cl miniature of Cointreau or
   other orange-flavoured liqueur
2 tbsp caster sugar
$1/2$ orange and $1/2$ lemon,
   finely sliced
$1/4$ of a ripe honeydew melon,
   peeled and cut into cubes
Chilled soda water to taste

Pour the wine into a large jug with the Cointreau and sugar and stir till the sugar has dissolved. Add the orange and lemon slices and leave to infuse for an hour or so. Add the melon and 10-12 ice cubes then top up with soda to taste.

What is life these days without lists? Here's how to find your favourite food.

BEST BEGINNERS

Easiest ever pasta sauce, *44*
Extremely easy stir-fry, *51*
Easy Italian tuna and bean
　salad, *60*
The best ever cheese on
　toast, *74*
No-carve roast chicken
　dinner, *128*

BEST LOW-FAT

Thai-style mackeral salad, *61*
Chinese steamed salmon
　with ginger, garlic and soy, *62*
Moroccan spiced carrot salad, *57*
Incredibly slimming cucumber
　salad, *31*
Asian-style low-fat dressing, *56*

BEST STONY-BROKE

Chunky potato, garlic and onion
　soup, *86*
Potato, bacon and onion
　frittata, *55*
Garlic mushrooms on toast, *75*
Spaghetti carbonara with peas, *47*
Chilli beef hash, *112*

BEST EXTRAVAGANT

Truffled mushroom risotto, *160*
Smoked salmon pizza with
　cream cheese and rocket, *168*

BEST VEGAN

BEST COMFORT

BEST HOT AND SPICY

BEST RECIPES WITH BOOZE

BEST SWEET TREATS